The Nine

Defining Markers of the Bible

Donnie Smith

Renown Publishing
www.renownpublishing.com

The Nine / Donnie Smith
ISBN-13: 978-1-952602-71-9

Acknowledgments

Kristina, noble character is found in you. You bring good, and your arms are always open. Your heart and eyes are unmatched. Thank you for your support, love, and laughs.

Kylie and Clayton, never follow your heart—always follow God. I'm proud of both of you. Please stay at the feet of Jesus while you are accomplishing great things in this big world.

Dad, your love and pride in me have allowed me to live a life without daddy issues. Thank you for giving me strength, humor, and guts to face the world. I miss them, too.

Peggy and Dwayne, thank you for being a steady ship. Your marriage, love for God, and youngest daughter have shaped my life.

To my Fellowship family—I am honored to be your pastor. Thank you for allowing me to be me. God has used you to make a massive spiritual dent in our cities!

To Brandon—I am honored that you would take part in this project. I'm even more honored that you've been a part of my life.

To Todd—thanks for all that you were willing to do to make this project better.

CONTENTS

CHAPTER ONE

Getting Oriented

I have sat down with many people to talk about the Bible over the years, and there seems to be a common theme: many people really struggle with Scripture. They struggle with how the Bible is organized, where to start reading, and what different passages mean. Reading Scripture isn't encouraging or enlightening for them—it's frustrating, exhausting, and overwhelming.

Maybe this is where you are. Maybe you avoid reading and studying Scripture, diving deep into it, because you can't connect all the pieces. Trust me, I understand this.

At some point in our lives, we all get that one phone call that makes the world stand still. The news on the other end of the line might be the highlight of your life, or it might serve as the darkest moment. Either way, you will remember it forever, and your life will never be the same. I was thirteen when I received a call that changed something inside of me. I have had several since then, but this particular call was the first, and its memory never escapes me. In fact, the events around this call helped shape my desire to dig into the specifics of God's story and how it is organized.

It was a typical mid-summer day in Oklahoma. The sound of my phone ringing woke me from a deep, teen-aged sleep. I rolled over to pick up the phone and muttered some form of greeting that was supposed to be hello into the phone. Whatever I managed to mumble was plenty to light the fuse on the other end of the line, where I heard the voice of my best friend, Joey. In typical "Joey" fashion, he gave an over-exaggerated "*Dude!*" and said, "Wake up!"

"What?" I managed, just in time for him to start a rant.

"You are not going to believe this. I can't believe this!" he exclaimed.

"What? What happened?" I said.

The only response he gave was, "Meet me in the middle right now!" I knew what that meant. We lived about a half-mile apart and we always met halfway—the middle.

So, I hung up the phone, jumped out of bed, and got on my bike. I rode hard to get there as fast as I could, convinced he was going to be showing off his new bike, or maybe even a new puppy. My mind was racing as fast as my legs were peddling. When I approached "the middle," I saw him crest the hill. He was on his bike waving something in the air. I couldn't tell what he was waving, but he was yelling incessantly, trying to tell me what was going on.

We were finally close enough for me to see that the bike he was riding was the same dented, scratched bike he'd had forever, so I knew that was not what all the excitement was about. I still didn't know what all the yelling was for, but I saw he had a newspaper in his hand. Crashing into our meeting spot, he was talking so loud and fast, it was incomprehensible. His mind blazed forward while his words struggled to catch up. I simply said, "Slow down! What are you talking about?"

Stopping long enough to catch his breath, he said, "Okay, do you remember the girl from yesterday?"

As soon as he said those words, *"the girl from yesterday,"* my heart started beating fast and chills spread over my body. My stomach churned, and fear took over me. Joey was referring to someone I will never forget.

Let me back up a little. Joey and I had a local waterpark near our houses that was a popular summer hangout for families and teens. One of many things this waterpark had was a giant pool. On one side of the pool, there was a shallow area with waterfalls and splash pads, and on the other side was a giant tower with a zip line that landed in the deeper end of the pool. That was the setting for the story of "the girl from yesterday."

The day before, we were in that very pool and saw a girl hovering just above the floor of the pool. Joey swam down and could tell she wasn't conscious. He then went under to grab her, swam her back up to the surface, and began to yell for help. The lifeguards pulled her out of the pool and cleared the area. We gathered with the large crowd, being pushed back further and further until we could no longer see what was going on. As the day went on, stories about what had happened were the talk of the waterpark.

As our sunburns deepened by the minute, so did the rumors, and the supposed outcome of the girl grew murkier. So, when Joey said, "Do you remember the girl from yesterday?"—of course I did. I could never forget that day. After receiving my affirmation that I recollected the most dramatic day I had experienced at that point in my life, Joey said, "They got it all wrong!"

The news had hit the press, but the story was missing details. The article that led to our early morning meeting was out of order and missing key elements. The timeline was wrong, the location was wrong, and Joey—the hero of the story—was never even mentioned. The people in our city would be reading an article that only told them part of the story, and they would miss out on feeling the things they should feel about it.

The real story had a dramatic timeline, a specific popular location, trauma, and even a local hero, but the report was written without any of that. A great story never misses the details. A great story is organized so the audience can see the whole picture. A great story tells the truth.

The article Joey was waving in the air is how most people see the Bible—as information with only a few details. God's Word is so much more than information with a little detail thrown in! It is the most wonderful book ever written, and it is not missing anything. God didn't write an article for us. God wrote a great story giving us a detailed account of who He is, who we are, why we are here, and where we ultimately will go. God organized His story in such a way that we can step into the pages and feel it fully, truly experiencing Him. We just have to figure out how to navigate the gift of His Word.

My goal in this book is to give you nine markers in the

Bible that will take you all the way through Scripture and help you understand God's Word from beginning to end.

Finding Your Bearings in Scripture

Let's start with some background on the Bible. Do you know what the word *Bible* means? It's the Greek word for "book."[1] The Holy Bible is therefore the holy book. The Bible is made up of the Old Testament and the New Testament. There are thirty-nine books in the Old Testament, which tells the story of the world before Jesus walked on earth, and the twenty-seven books in the New Testament tell the story of what happened when Jesus was on earth and after He left.

The Bible was written over the course of fifteen hundred years by forty different authors, all under the inspiration of the Holy Spirit, on three different continents: Asia, Africa, and Europe.[2]

It's been out in the open for well over two thousand years, and plenty of people have tried to shoot holes in it, looking for factual errors or otherwise trying to disprove it. And they have not been able to do it. In fact, the longer the Bible is in existence, the more it is revealed to be true. As more history is discovered and more archaeological finds are dug up, God's Word is proven to be accurate and authentic.[3]

I find this fascinating because even though many Christians recognize the Bible as the Word of God, we don't always understand that it is truly the Word *of* God. To comprehend and capture the fullness of Scripture, we have to *see* the fullness of Scripture. God Himself has organized His Word for our benefit. So let's explore the organization of Scripture using nine markers that will benefit us as we study God's Word and live out His story.

The first marker is *creation*. Genesis 1:1 tells us, "In the beginning, God created the heavens and the earth." God created. This was no accident. He intentionally created the heavens and the earth, and then He intentionally created man and woman and placed them in the garden. He gave them the perfect world, the perfect scenario, and they had perfect union and communion with Him.

The second marker is *the fall*. Adam and Eve were living in the garden, and God told them that there was one tree in the garden that they were not to eat from—the tree of the knowledge of good and evil (Genesis 2:16–17). Everything else was theirs. God encouraged them to find pleasure in everything else but not to eat from this one tree. What did Adam and Eve do? They ate from that one tree. They sinned against God, which separated them from God and broke their relationship with Him.

The third marker is *the Law*. As a result of the fall, God had to manage what had taken place. Sin had entered the world; the Law had to be established to control it. Sin broke what God had created, so God put a cast on His creation to help it heal. This cast was the Law, and it would remain on humanity until Jesus, the Healer, would come.

The fourth marker is the *judges*. Let's think about the Law for a moment. If you knew there were no police officers out on the road, would you drive the speed limit? Most of us probably wouldn't. Someone had to oversee the Law, so God established the judges for the purpose of overseeing the Law and leading God's people.

The fifth marker is the *kings*. God's people had a problem with the judges; they didn't want judges. They wanted to be led by a king, and when history unfolded, a king is what God gave them. But then there was a problem with the kings. Their actions divided the nation and led to war and instability where there was supposed to be peace. Everything was fractured and torn, and it all began to crumble.

The sixth marker is the *prophets*. The prophets spoke to God and then delivered that message to the people, sharing what God told them. They talked about creation, sin, the fall of man, and the Law. The prophets also shared about the judges and the kings.

The main purpose of the prophets, however, was not to speak about what had transpired but to proclaim what was yet to come. Isaiah 52–53, for example, goes into great detail about the death of Jesus Christ—seven hundred years before Jesus walked on the earth.[4] Isaiah 53:5 tells us that He "was pierced for our transgressions" and "crushed for our iniquities; upon him was the chastisement that brought us peace, and with his wounds we are healed." It even mentions that Jesus will be placed in a rich man's tomb (Isaiah 53:9). How did Isaiah know these things? Because God was speaking to Isaiah and sharing these things with him.

The prophets said there would ultimately be one king, the King of kings. This King will not divide nations but will reconcile people back to Himself. The prophets proclaimed the hero of the Bible, the point of all of Scripture, *Jesus*.

The seventh marker is *Jesus*. Jesus lived on the earth

for thirty-three years.[5] He walked, He loved, and He served. It's interesting we have so much difficulty understanding and following His teachings, because He made Himself very clear.

After thirty-three years on earth, Jesus was hung on Calvary's cross. He was placed in a borrowed tomb, and three days later, He resurrected. Once He rose, Jesus spent forty days on earth. Before ascending to the Father, He said to His disciples, "Go therefore and make disciples of all nations, baptizing them in the name of the Father and of the Son and of the Holy Spirit, teaching them to observe all that I have commanded you. And behold, I am with you always, to the end of the age" (Matthew 28:19–20).

The eighth marker is *the church.* In addition to doing a work on the cross to re-establish the relationship with God for which mankind was created, Jesus established His church. The purpose of the church is not just for us to come together and live in community but also for us to be God's people and reach the world.

The ninth marker is *the promise of Jesus' return*. He promised the church He would return for His people. In John 14:2–3, Jesus said, "In my Father's house are many rooms. If it were not so, would I have told you that I go to prepare a place for you? And if I go and prepare a place for you, I will come again and will take you to myself, that where I am you may be also."

Jesus did not promise He will return again for the world or to take away sin again—He already accomplished all of that on the cross. He did promise that He is going to return for the church and bring us home to be with Him. This is a promise for us, and in order to believe that promise, we need to understand Scripture. We need to *know* the fullness of Scripture so we can *comprehend* the fullness of Scripture.

It's Time to Start Your Journey

Here is the organization of the Bible: creation, the fall, the Law, judges, kings, prophets, Jesus, the church, and the promise of Jesus' return. It doesn't seem complicated, does it? You can do this. By following these nine markers in the Bible, you will be able to navigate Scripture to understand who God is, who we are, why we are here, and where we ultimately will go.

In the nine chapters that follow, we will walk systematically through Scripture, taking a deep dive into each of the nine markers to help you better understand the fullness of God's Word. At the end of each chapter, workbook sections will guide you to explore these nine markers more fully in your personal life. My prayer for you is, by the end of this book, you will not only have a deeper understanding of the Bible but will also have fallen in love with Scripture.

God's Word is a lamp to our feet and a light to our path (Psalm 119:105). Like the phone call that led me to the rendezvous with Joey, the Word helps us realize how many details are missing from the story the rest of the world tells us. Identifying the nine markers will help us learn how to find our way through Scripture, developing a greater comprehension of what God wants to do in us and through us. We will never again read only part of the story!

Chapter One Notes

CHAPTER TWO

Creation

The first marker that will help us to navigate through Scripture is creation. Genesis 1:1 tells us, "In the beginning, God created the heavens and the earth." In the discussion of creation, there are so many directions we could go. We must establish these two things regarding creation: 1) that it was God who created and 2) how He feels about His creation.

At this point in Scripture, God had not yet given us His name. He was still the Alpha and the Omega, the beginning and the end.[6] The Hebrew word for God in Genesis 1:1 is *Elohim*, which is more of a general term for a god.[7] It was not God's name.

Where did God's *name* come from? His name is a Hebrew word that means "lord," and it comes from the word *Yahweh.*[8] This word was established to identify God, and it appears more than six thousand times in the Old Testament.[9]

The word *Yahweh* is so sacred, so holy to the Jewish people, that before they wrote God's name, they would wash their hands and pray. They would use special symbols to write out His name, and then they would wash their hands again and repent. They had so much respect for His name that it seemed irreverent to write it out, let alone use it in vain.

When God created Adam and Eve and put them in the garden of Eden, He gave them the distinct honor of naming the animals. But who gave God His name? Where did it come from? It comes from Exodus 3:13–14, when God was speaking with Moses:

> *Then Moses said to God, "If I come to the people of Israel and say to them, 'The God of your fathers has sent me to you,' and they ask me, 'What is his name?' what shall I say to them?" God said to Moses, "I AM WHO I AM." And he said, "Say this to the people of Israel: 'I AM has sent me to you.'"*

And thus, God's name was established, and He established it Himself. "I AM" is the Hebrew word *Yahweh*. *Yahweh* also means "lord," and it means "God." All three meanings are synonymous. And this God is our creator. He is the one who spoke all things into existence and created Adam as man in His image. Eve was created in the same image, to be the helpmate. When God created Adam and Eve, He created them to walk in communion with Him—to have relationship with Him. When God spoke all things into existence, all the beauty of the earth and splendor of the animals, God chose to give man dominion over them.

So, how does God feel about His creation? He loves us, but let's let Isaiah answer that question in greater detail.

Isaiah was a prophet, which means God spoke to him and through him about the past, the present, and the future—and we will see all three in the following verses.

> *But now thus says the LORD, he who created you, O Jacob, he who formed you, O Israel: "Fear not, for I have redeemed you; I have called you by name, you are mine."*
>
> ***—Isaiah 43:1***

Israel is the name that God changed Jacob's name to, as he was the father of the twelve tribes of Israel (Genesis 32:22–32). That's the part of the scripture that focuses on the past. God makes it clear in this verse, we are His. We belong to Him, and He is jealous over us.

I'm reminded of the time I went to play golf with my son and I lost my favorite pair of sunglasses. I didn't realize they were missing until late at night. I ran out to my car to see if I had left them in there, but there was no sign of them. I was in a total panic. These are expensive sunglasses, and I'm very careful not to lose them. I was so distraught that I could barely sleep.

First thing in the morning, I called the golf course to see if anyone found my glasses. There was no sign of them. Now, I know enough about golf courses to know that the first person out on the green each day is the guy who does the mowing. And if no one found shards of broken sunglasses on the tenth hole, chances are the mower stole them.

I was up in arms over the possibility that someone stole my precious sunglasses, and I asked if they could check with the mower to see if he had come across them. Nope, the mower hadn't seen them.

Later that day, my son and I went back to the golf course to practice. I combed the green for my sunglasses while we played, and all of a sudden, I saw them—on someone else's face!

Maybe he just had the same pair of sunglasses I did? Something in my gut told me to go over to this guy and ask.

But as soon as I started walking toward him, he started walking in a different direction. I could see where he was headed, so I took a shortcut and caught up with him. As soon as he saw me, he changed direction again. I was chasing him around the golf course at this point.

I caught up with him again as he came around a corner, and I noticed he was now wearing a completely different pair of sunglasses. He knew I was on to him, and he was trying to hide the evidence.

I wasn't about to let him get away with it, though. This guy stole my favorite sunglasses! So, I walked right up to him and engaged him in conversation in a firm, hey-I'm-a-pastor tone of voice, and I convinced him to give me back my sunglasses.

He acted as though it had been a mistake, like he had just found the glasses and didn't know they belonged to me, but I knew what had really happened. And let me tell you, I have never been so excited to have my sunglasses.

Those were my sunglasses, and I chased a total stranger around a golf course to get them back. God created us, and He says that we are His. Is it any surprise that when we run away from Him, He chases us down to get us back? Is it any surprise He wants us? We are His! This is how He feels about us, His creation—that we are His.

Listen to how serious God is about this. He continues in Isaiah 43:2: "When you pass through the waters, I will be with you; and through the rivers, they shall not overwhelm you; when you walk through fire you shall not be burned, and the flame shall not consume you."

This is God telling us that we are His but also that He is with us. This is a reference to the past—how He was with His people during the Exodus and how He was with Shadrach, Meshach, and Abednego in the furnace—but it is also a promise for the present and the future.

How great a promise is this for us today? God is with us. He will not leave us. Sometimes you might feel like you do things that are bad and make God run away from you, but He does not run away from you. He runs toward you, and He walks with you. In the New Testament, Jesus used an example that exposed His love for His people: when a sheep is lost, He goes after them (Luke 15). In the Old Testament, Psalm 139:7–10, we see that there is nowhere to run from God. There is no reason even to attempt to run from God, because there is nowhere you can hide from Him and His love.

God continued in Isaiah 43:3, "For I am the LORD your God, the Holy One of Israel, your Savior. I give Egypt as your ransom, Cush and Seba in exchange for you." He told us in Isaiah 43:1 that we are His, and He told us in this verse that He is ours. He created us so we could be His and He could be ours. Through Isaiah, God was putting the pieces together and explaining why He created us.

Have you ever noticed, when God has something important to say in Scripture, He repeats Himself? Look at what Jesus said in John 5:24: "Truly, truly, I say to you, whoever hears my word and believes him who sent me has eternal life. He does not come into judgment, but has passed from death to life." When Jesus says, "Truly, truly," He was really saying, "You'd better listen."

And consider what the seraphim say as they hover above God's throne in Isaiah 6:3, "Holy, holy, holy is the LORD of hosts; the whole earth is full of his glory!" The seraphim want to make sure we understand that God is holy.

Seeing now what repetition in God's Word means, pay attention! God had just told His people they were His in Isaiah 43:1, and He told them again He was theirs in Isaiah 43:3: "For I am the LORD your God, the Holy One of Israel, your Savior. I give Egypt as your ransom." Now let's put some of the original Hebrew in there: "For *Yahweh* the *Yahweh* your *Yahweh.*"

That's some serious repetition. God wants us to understand that He is our God and that He means what He says. We are His, and He is ours. And He is not going to run from us.

Why? "Because you are precious in my eyes, and honored, and I love you" (Isaiah 43:4). This is the Creator of the universe saying to us, "You are mine, and I am yours, and I love you."

Maybe you don't know what it feels like to be loved, because this world has lied to you. When you hear God loves you, you don't know how to receive it. We live in a world filled with hate, but we serve a God who created us and is filled with love for us.

God continued in Isaiah 43:5–6: "Fear not, for I am

with you; I will bring your offspring from the east, and from the west I will gather you. I will say to the north, Give up, and to the south, Do not withhold; bring my sons from afar and my daughters from the end of the earth." Remember, this was Isaiah speaking on God's behalf as a prophet and sharing what God had told him. Isaiah was speaking to the present time, but he was also speaking more broadly.

The book of Judges, which is about events before Isaiah's time, was characterized by sin cycles. The people would sin, and God would redeem them and restore them. During a later sin cycle, about which Isaiah prophesied in this scripture, the Babylonians came and took God's people into exile, scattering them all around. Isaiah was speaking in this particular text about how God would bring the exiles back from Babylon and reconcile them to Himself.

Isaiah could speak with a wider scope than his present experience, or even his people's past, because he was speaking on behalf of the Alpha and the Omega. God knows the past, the present, and the future. This scripture points both to what they were going through and to what will happen at the second coming of Jesus, when God's people will be gathered and reunited. They will be reconciled to a holy and righteous God.

Where does that future interpretation come from? It comes from the verse's context. In this passage, who was exiled to Babylon? According to Isaiah 43:1, it was the Israelites, as seen in the fact that God was addressing Jacob and Israel.

But then, there is a shift in the language when we get to Isaiah 43:5–7:

> *Fear not, for I am with you; I will bring your offspring from the east, and from the west I will gather you. I will say to the north, Give up, and to the south, Do not withhold; bring my sons from afar and my daughters from the end of the earth, everyone who is called by my name, whom I created for my glory, whom I formed and made.*

By the time we reach verse 7, God was no longer just addressing Israel. He was addressing everyone who is called by His name. John 3:16 tells us, "For God so loved the world, that he gave his only Son, that whoever believes in him should not perish but have eternal life." In the original Greek form and the original Hebrew form, "whoever" in John 3:16 and "everyone" in Isaiah 43:7 have the same meaning, which is the word *everyone*.[10] These verses in Isaiah 43 start by addressing Israel and their restoration from exile, but they end with God promising to gather all His people—*everyone* who is called by His name—at the second coming of Jesus Christ.

Created to Bring God Glory

Why did God create? Isaiah 43:7 states that we were created for God's glory. We were created for a purpose, and that purpose is God's glory.

All of creation reveals God's glory. Psalm 19:1 tells us, "The heavens declare the glory of God, and the sky above proclaims his handiwork." Go out into the deep country on a cloudless night and look up at the stars. How can you not see God's glory? Go to the foothills of a mountain and gaze up at the snow-covered peaks, or go to the ocean to watch the sun set while the waves splash over your feet. It all just screams of God's glory.

We find it easy to believe that nature was created for God's glory, but God wants us to take it a step further and understand that we ourselves were also created for His glory. Isaiah 43:7 says that every*one* was created for His glory. Do you understand what that means? *You* were created for God's glory! Genesis 1:27 says, "So God created man in his own image, in the image of God he created him; male and female he created them." Therefore, there are eight billion people on this earth, all created to bear God's glory.

Humanity as a whole does not bear the glory of God. His glory is not always reflected in humanity because of sin, and thus, we no longer believe that we are able to reflect His glory. Instead of allowing the Word of God to define us, we have bought into the lies of the world, which means all that defines us is our sin. Our identity is based on our failures and mistakes rather than on the reality that we are God's image-bearers who were created to glorify Him.

When you look in the mirror, you should see God's glory reflected in you just as you see it reflected in nature. You are glorious. You were created to glorify a holy and righteous God in everything you do and everything you say.

But what's devastating is this: God created us for His glory, and that glory has been shattered by sin. The glory we are supposed to be able to reflect through our lives has been damaged. It's like looking into a broken mirror. You can't see an accurate reflection because of all the cracks and fractures. As a result, we are no longer the glorious image-bearers we were created to be.

But as we work our way through Scripture, we will see there is hope. Do not buy the lies of the world. Do not settle for being identified by your mistakes and failures. Refuse to be defined by what the world says about you or what other people say about you.

God created you for His glory; therefore, His Word defines you. Creation spells out that you are His, He is yours, and He created you for His glory.

WORKBOOK

Chapter Two Questions

Question: What is your response to the fact that God created you and that He wants you?

Action: Below, create two columns. In one column, list the lies of this world—the things that the world or others say about you when trying to define you by your mistakes, failures, shortcomings, etc. In the other column, list the truth God speaks over your life about who you are to Him and who He has called you to be.

____

____

____

____

____

____

____

____

____

____

____

____

Chapter Two Notes

CHAPTER THREE

The Fall

The second marker that will help us to navigate through Scripture is the fall of mankind, living outside of what we were created for: God's glory. It would be wonderful if bringing God glory came easy—if God's glory were a natural response. Unfortunately, we all have a sin nature coming directly from the original fall.

One day I came home from work and my wife had both of our children sitting in the middle of the kitchen floor. My daughter at the time was six, and my son was three. The dilemma was that Oreos had disappeared. My wife knew she hadn't eaten them, and both children were denying that they had eaten the cookies. But my wife, knowing that sin nature comes naturally, was convinced one of them was lying. She was not going to let them move from the kitchen floor until they told her the truth.

Now, we never had to teach our kids to lie or how to eat cookies when they were not supposed to. In other words, she was trying to teach them to work against their fallen sin nature and tell the truth.

Well, I ruined the entire teaching moment because I had to pull my wife into the next room to tell her to cut them slack. Before I could finish, she cut me off and told me that it's our job to teach them honesty, so I couldn't let them get away with this lie. I slowly lifted my finger and placed it over her mouth, leaned into her ear, and whispered, "I ate the Oreos."

It was an awkward parenting moment for both of us, but my wife was operating in what we all know: sin comes naturally, and the fall left a mark on each of us. For us to understand the fullness of Scripture, we must understand sin and what it has done to us. This is a key part of understanding God's glory and His redemptive story.

If I were to take a poll and ask people, "What is sin?" the majority might respond that sin is doing bad things. They might define sin as breaking God's law or breaking God's rules. That is correct, but there's more to it.

Yes, Scripture is full of things we should and should not do for the glory of God. But those do's and don'ts do not necessarily give us the complete definition of sin.

Here's an example. Would you consider it a sin for someone to wear a hat? Of course not. Would you consider it a sin for someone to write on a piece of paper? Again, of course not. When someone's favorite college football team scores a touchdown, is it a sin for them to get excited and wave a flag? None of these things are sin.

But what if someone is wearing a hat with a hateful message on it, holding a poster on which they have written a hateful slogan, and waving a flag in support of an unbiblical cause? The sin is not necessarily in the hat, the poster, or the flag. It's in the heart of the person who is embracing hatred and bigotry and using these objects as tools to reflect that. The sin is what exists inside of them.

We need to understand the depravity of man and how we ended up this way. God created us for His glory, but we have destroyed it through sin.

Sin Brings Death

We see the origins of sin begin to unfold in Genesis 2:15–17:

> *The LORD God took the man and put him in the garden of Eden to work it and keep it. And the LORD God commanded the man, saying, "You may surely eat of every tree of the garden, but of the tree of the knowledge of good and evil you shall not eat, for in the day that you eat of it you shall surely die."*

In the original Hebrew of verse 17, God did not say, "*If* you eat of this tree, you shall surely die." Instead, the wording is more like, "*When* you eat of it…." He said, "for in the day that you eat of it…." God knew what was going to happen here.

Scripture continues to point us to the reality that sin leads to death. Romans 6:23 states, "For the wages of sin is death, but the free gift of God is eternal life in Christ Jesus our Lord." Romans 3:23 takes it a step further in saying, "For all have sinned and fall short of the glory of God." This is the picture we're looking at: God created us for His glory, but all of us have sinned and fallen short of that glory, our intended purpose.

God warned Adam in the garden that if he ate the fruit of the tree of the knowledge of good and evil, he would no longer be a bearer of the glory of God, and death would reign. Surely Adam and Eve would have understood that God was telling them the truth and, therefore, refrained from eating fruit off of that tree. But we know how the story goes:

> *Now the serpent was more crafty than any other beast of the field that the LORD God had made. He said to the woman, "Did God actually say, 'You shall not eat of any tree in the garden'?" And the woman said to the serpent, "We may eat of the fruit of the trees in the garden, but God said, 'You shall not eat of the fruit of the tree that is in the midst of the garden, neither shall you touch it, lest you die.'" But the serpent said to the woman, "You will not surely die. For God knows that when you eat of it your eyes will be opened, and you will be like God, knowing good and evil." So when the woman saw that the tree was good for food, and that it was a delight to the eyes, and that the tree was to be desired to make one wise, she took of its fruit and ate, and she also gave some to her husband who was with her, and he ate. Then the eyes of both were opened, and they knew that they were naked. And they sewed fig leaves together and made themselves loincloths.*
>
> ***—Genesis 3:1–7***

Adam and Eve did not listen to God's warning. They chose instead to believe the serpent that God didn't say what He said, and if He did say what He said, He didn't really mean it.

God then came to see Adam and Eve, and He asked them what happened: "The man said, 'The woman whom you gave to be with me, she gave me fruit of the tree, and

I ate.' Then the LORD God said to the woman, 'What is this that you have done?' The woman said, 'The serpent deceived me, and I ate'" (Genesis 3:12–13).

Adam blamed Eve, and Eve blamed the serpent. None of us really want to come to grips with our own sin. We want to blame it on everyone else so that we don't have to take responsibility for our actions. It's all too easy to play the blame game.

Remember, God told them that when they ate the fruit of that tree, they would die. Did Adam and Eve drop dead at that very moment? No. But does that mean God was wrong? No. What it means is, though we immediately see the obvious consequences of sin, the spiritual death is separation from God. God created man to walk in perfect union with Him, but because of sin, there was now an immediate separation. We begin to see, from the fall of Adam and Eve onward, the consequences of sin and the devastation of the separation from God.

In Genesis 4, Cain, Adam and Eve's firstborn, became a murderer. Genesis 5 records the deaths of Adam and his descendants up to Noah. In Genesis 6–8, we see mankind becoming increasingly depraved and hardening their hearts against God, culminating in the flood and God wiping the earth clean of wickedness and sin.

Romans 5:12 makes it absolutely clear: "Therefore, just as sin came into the world through one man, and death through sin, and so death spread to all men because all sinned." Death is a consequence of sin. Each and every one of us will face the reality of ourselves dying. There are no exceptions.

Sin Brings God's Wrath

It's not just that sin brought death. Sin also brought God's wrath, and His wrath is revealed in Scripture in a way that many of us ignore. This is because we all still sin. And if we really believed sin leads to death and it brings the wrath of God, we might not make some of the choices we make. Romans 1:18–23 explains God's wrath like this:

> *For the wrath of God is revealed from heaven against all ungodliness and unrighteousness of men, who by their unrighteousness suppress the truth. For what can be known about God is plain to them, because God has shown it to them. For his invisible attributes, namely, his eternal power and divine nature, have been clearly perceived, ever since the creation of the world, in the things that have been made. So they are without excuse. For although they knew God, they did not honor him as God or give thanks to him, but they became futile in their thinking, and their foolish hearts were darkened. Claiming to be wise, they became fools, and exchanged the glory of the immortal God for images resembling mortal man and birds and animals and creeping things.*

They exchanged the glory of God—the glory for which they were created—for their own desires. This is no different from your story or my story. We were created for the purpose of bringing God glory, and yet our desires lead us down a road that is completely contrary to that.

The people mentioned in this passage from Romans thought they were wise, but they were really fools. Do you know what the real sin was in the garden of Eden? Yes, there was the sin of disobeying God by doing what He told them not to do, but there was an underlying heart issue as well. Up until that point, Adam and Eve had only known good, but by eating from that tree, they would also know evil. That was the heart issue, the real sin: Adam and Eve wanted to be the ones to determine right and wrong.

By taking that fruit, they were taking away God's authority to say what is good and what is evil, what is right and what is wrong. They wanted the authority to determine what is right and wrong in their own lives. This sinful desire was the core of their hearts, and it was more devastating than the sin of disobedience.

How many people do you know who ignore the authority of God's Word and insist they have the right to make their own choices? How many people do you know who refuse to accept Scripture as their ultimate authority and the standard for what is right and what is wrong? So many of us have left our Bible on the shelf to gather dust and come up with our own definitions of right and wrong. We do the same thing Adam and Eve did.

Sin brings death and God's wrath, and it's all because of our foolishness. The choices we make are determined by what we believe. If we do not believe sin brings the wrath of God, then we will choose to continue to sin. We will exchange God's glory for God's wrath by choosing our own will and our own way instead of God's will and God's way.

And you were dead in the trespasses and sins in which you once walked, following the course of this world, following the prince of the power of the air, the spirit that is now at

> *work in the sons of disobedience—among whom we all once lived in the passions of our flesh, carrying out the desires of the body and the mind, and were by nature children of wrath, like the rest of mankind.*
>
> ***—Ephesians 2:1–3***

God created everything that exists for His glory, and He created us to be His children. But because of sin, not all of us are children of God. The world would like us to think all people are children of God, but that is a lie. We are all God's creation, but we are not God's children until we are covered by the cross and have been redeemed. You cannot be called God's child until this sin issue has been dealt with, and Jesus alone fixes our sin issue—not the Law, the judges, the kings, or the prophets. Just Jesus. Only Jesus dealt with our sin.

And sin doesn't only bring death and wrath. It goes deeper than that. In those verses from Ephesians 2, Paul made it clear there is a problem with our hearts, which is reflected in the desires of our bodies and our minds.

Jesus Shields Us from Death and Wrath

But I don't want to leave you hopeless. As we continue to study the redemptive story of God, we will eventually reach that healing moment Jesus offers. In the meantime, I'd like to encourage you with 2 Thessalonians 1:6–10:

> *Since indeed God considers it just to repay with affliction those who afflict you, and to grant relief to you who are afflicted as well as to us, when the Lord Jesus is revealed from heaven with his mighty angels in flaming fire, inflicting*

> *vengeance on those who do not know God and on those who do not obey the gospel of our Lord Jesus. They will suffer the punishment of eternal destruction, away from the presence of the Lord and from the glory of his might, when he comes on that day to be glorified in his saints, and to be marveled at among all who have believed, because our testimony to you was believed.*

Because of sin, God's wrath is coming. When Jesus returns, He is coming with flames and an army of angels to inflict vengeance on His creation that has sinned against Him. These people will suffer God's wrath because they are His creation, not His children, and they are therefore not under His protection until they are under the protection of Christ.

Those who are apart from Christ will have no protection from His wrath. But those who are in Christ will be protected. We saw this happen at Passover in Exodus 12, when those with blood on their door were passed over. It will happen again when Jesus returns in vengeance with His angels. Everything will be consumed by that fiery vengeance—except for those of us who are able to hide behind the shield of the cross. That vengeance, that wrath, will be deflected by the shield that is Jesus.

If you are in Christ, God's wrath will not consume you. That's why Romans 8:1 says, "There is therefore now no condemnation for those who are in Christ Jesus."

John 3:36 makes it clear: "Whoever believes in the Son has eternal life, whoever does not obey the Son shall not see life, but the wrath of God remains on him." Without Christ, we will never live out the glory we were created for. Again, our sin not only brings death, but it also brings

God's wrath. Those who believe in Christ will not see wrath, but life. That's a promise. Those who do not believe in Christ will never see life—only wrath.

Sin Is a Heart Issue

Remember, all of us have sinned and fallen short of the glory of God (Romans 3:23). Whether your sins seem small and inconsequential to you or your sins seem like they are threatening to overwhelm you, sin is sin. It doesn't matter how small or how big the sin is. All sins are equal because they still separate you from God.

But just like with Adam and Eve in the garden of Eden, your sin itself isn't the core issue. The core issue is your heart. Sin doesn't just bring death and God's wrath. It also brings the hardening of our hearts. If you're a Christ-follower, every time you sin against God, the Holy Spirit who lives inside you convicts you. But if we suppress the Holy Spirit and do not allow Him to nurture and mold us, our heart gets a little bit harder.

And if we continue to do that, we become people with hardened hearts. It doesn't matter how regularly we attend church, how good we think we are, or how much volunteer work we do; we are still living sinful lives because our hearts are hard, and we are not honoring God.

This is our daily struggle. We are born with a sinful nature, and we have to do battle with it every day so that sin nature is not what defines our story. We must acknowledge Christ has redeemed our souls and we belong to the Lord. Our mindset should be that we are going to do everything in our power to exemplify Christ.

Take a look at Jesus' teachings. In John 8, the scribes and the Pharisees brought to Jesus a woman who was caught in adultery and demanded to know if they should stone her as the Law commanded. Jesus responded, "Let him who is without sin among you be the first to throw a stone at her" (John 8:7). When no one stepped forward to do so, Jesus told the woman to go and sin no more (John 8:11).

Jesus wasn't saying it was okay for the woman to sin. And He certainly made it clear to the scribes and the Pharisees that they needed to check their hearts. Jesus wasn't dealing with what people were doing; He was dealing with their hearts. Our objective as believers is to have a soft heart before God. We have all sinned and fallen short of God's glory, but we were created for God's glory and redeemed for God's glory, and now we need to make choices every day that will display God's glory through our lives.

WORKBOOK

Chapter Three Questions

Question: What do you understand sin to be? How does God define sin in His Word?

____

____

____

____

____

____

____

____

____

____

____

Action: Make a list of negative consequences you have experienced from sin in your life. What does that reveal to you about God's heart and why He wants you not to sin?

____

____

____

____

____

____

____

____

____

____

____

____

Chapter Three Notes

CHAPTER FOUR

The Law

The third marker that will help us to navigate through Scripture is the Law. We think of the Law as the dos and don'ts, a list of rules we must obey. To us, the Law in Scripture is punishment, because if we break the Law, we are punished. But that's a one-dimensional way of looking at the Law and its purpose.

My family and I took a road trip, and we were driving down the highway when we came up behind a police car in the right lane. The police car was going under the speed limit, and I could pass it safely without going over the speed limit by moving into the left lane, as is standard procedure. My wife warned me not to, but I argued that it wouldn't be breaking any rules for me to pass the police car in this way.

The moment I passed the police car, its lights went on. I pulled over, and the police officer came over to my window. I asked him what the problem was, and he replied, "I'm not sure where you're from, but around here, people don't normally zoom around the police."

I explained that I had done nothing wrong—I hadn't exceeded the speed limit, I hadn't cut him off, I hadn't passed him in a no-passing zone—and that where I was from, there weren't any issues with passing a police car safely and in accordance with the rules.

After a bit of back and forth, the officer returned to his car, and my wife whispered to me that she was sure he was going to write me a ticket. But I hadn't done anything wrong! Why would he write me a ticket?

"Because you made him mad," my wife said.

This is how we think about the Law. Because we've done something that's against the Law from God's perspective, we're sure we're going to be punished. Let's take a closer look at the Law in Scripture to help us shift the mindset that it is not about being punished.

The Law in Scripture

The first five books of the Old Testament are called the *Torah*,[11] which is the Hebrew word for "law."[12] Genesis, Exodus, Leviticus, Numbers, and Deuteronomy are the books of the Torah, and they contain more than six hundred laws.[13] Those laws are divided into three categories: civil laws, ceremonial laws, and moral laws.

God gave the Jewish people civil laws to govern their society, but they certainly didn't include speed limits because cars hadn't been invented yet. And yet, we have speed limits today. So, how do we reconcile this?

Romans 13:1 says, "Let every person be subject to the governing authorities. For there is no authority except from God, and those that exist have been instituted by

God." When Jesus told His followers to make disciples of all nations (Matthew 28:19–20), He knew that they would be traveling to places that weren't governed by Hebrew civil laws.

This verse from Romans is a reminder to God's people that we are subject to the local laws and the local authorities in the place where we live. For example, if you're an American, even if you don't like the person who is the President of the United States, he is still your President because God has established him and put him in that position. You don't have to like him, but you are still subject to him.

Does this mean that the Hebrew civil laws no longer exist? Well, no. Civil laws in every country around the world find roots in the Ten Commandments, whether they recognize that or not. However, in America, we do not live under direct Hebrew civil law; we live under American civil law.

Next, we have the ceremonial laws. Once a year, the Hebrew people would gather their sacrifices to make atonement for their sins. When was the last time you came to church and saw someone cutting a lamb's throat in the parking lot so they could pour the lamb's blood on the church's altar? Never, I hope. We no longer live under the ceremonial laws. Hebrews 10:1–7, 10 explains why:

> *For since the law has but a shadow of the good things to come instead of the true form of these realities, it can never, by the same sacrifices that are continually offered every year, make perfect those who draw near. Otherwise, would they not have ceased to be offered, since the worshipers, having once been cleansed, would no longer have any*

> *consciousness of sins? But in these sacrifices there is a reminder of sins every year. For it is impossible for the blood of bulls and goats to take away sins. Consequently, when Christ came into the world, he said, "Sacrifices and offerings you have not desired, but a body have you prepared for me; in burnt offerings and sin offerings you have taken no pleasure. Then I said, 'Behold, I have come to do your will, O God, as it is written of me in the scroll of the book.'" ... And by that will we have been sanctified through the offering of the body of Jesus Christ once for all.*

The Hebrews had ceremonial laws because they did not yet have Jesus' death on the cross for their sins, once and for all. But we do have Jesus, and because He became our ceremonial sacrifice, we no longer live under the ceremonial laws.

The Law Leads to Love

The third and final category of laws is the moral law. These moral laws are still intact today. In the introductory chapter, we talked about how the Law is like a cast for sin. Mankind was broken by sin, and the Law was applied as a cast to get us to a point of healing.

To shift metaphors a bit, the Law is also a road that leads to the foot of the cross. When we recognize this, we will understand the Law is not punishment. Rather, the Law leads to love. Deuteronomy 30:6 states, "And the LORD your God will circumcise your heart and the heart of your offspring, so that you will love the LORD your God with all your heart and with all your soul, that you may live."

The design was this. God created us for His glory, but

sin entered the world. Sin, remember, is a heart issue. Adam and Eve wanted God's authority and to be able to determine what was right and wrong for themselves. They were no different from us. We all want to have our own opinions and our own rules.

The Law was put in place to bind our hearts so that they can heal, which is what God was saying in Deuteronomy 30:6. He made it clear to the Israelites that He was pursuing their hearts. The Law was not to punish them; it was to recapture their hearts.

Let's take a look at this conversation between Jesus and a wealthy young man in Matthew 19:16–22:

> *And behold, a man came up to him, saying, "Teacher, what good deed must I do to have eternal life?" And he said to him, "Why do you ask me about what is good? There is only one who is good. If you would enter life, keep the commandments." He said to him, "Which ones?" And Jesus said, "You shall not murder, You shall not commit adultery, You shall not steal, You shall not bear false witness, Honor your father and mother, and, You shall love your neighbor as yourself." The young man said to him, "All these I have kept. What do I still lack?" Jesus said to him, "If you would be perfect, go, sell what you possess and give to the poor, and you will have treasure in heaven; and come, follow me." When the young man heard this he went away sorrowful, for he had great possessions.*

The wealthy young man had followed the rules. He had checked all the boxes on the list Jesus gave him, but his heart was still broken. Jesus encouraged him to take his eyes off the rules and look at his heart, at what was going on inside of him. The Law was not established to give us a to-do list. It was established to lead us to love—and not just to love ourselves.

Matthew 22:34–40 explains:

> *But when the Pharisees heard that [Jesus] had silenced the Sadducees, they gathered together. And one of them, a lawyer, asked him a question to test him. "Teacher, which is the great commandment in the Law?" And he said to him, "You shall love the Lord your God with all your heart and with all your soul and with all your mind. This is the great and first commandment. And a second is like it: You shall love your neighbor as yourself. On these two commandments depend all the Law and the Prophets."*

Jesus quoted Deuteronomy 6:5 on loving God and Leviticus 19 on loving your neighbor. The entire law points to the importance of loving God and loving your neighbor. If you love God and you love people, you are fulfilling the Law.

Romans 13:8–10 tells us:

> *Owe no one anything, except to love each other, for the one who loves another has fulfilled the law. For the commandments, "You shall not commit adultery, You shall not murder, You shall not steal, You shall not covet," and any other commandment, are summed up in this word: "You shall love your neighbor as yourself." Love does no wrong to a neighbor; therefore love is the fulfilling of the law.*

The Law was not established so we would feel like we were being punished. It was established so we would understand the depths of God's love for us.

The Law Leads to Faith

The Law does not lead only to love. It also leads to faith. Adam and Eve wanted to know what was right and what was wrong, and the Law was put in place to tell them what was right and what was wrong. God took back the authority Adam and Eve so desperately wanted and laid out for them what was good and what was evil.

Let me be clear: if you are in Christ, God is not going to punish you for your sins. You will experience the consequences of your sins, but God is not going to punish you for doing something wrong.

When you sin, you are to confess your sins to Jesus. Romans 8:1 tells us, "There is therefore now no condemnation for those who are in Christ Jesus." This means when you are in Christ, the judgment and punishment you fear will not come upon you. Yes, you will experience the consequences of your sin. Sin ruins and destroys lives, and there's no getting around it. But you will not be punished by God because you've done something wrong. That's not the way He operates.

There is punishment coming, and God has warned us about it. His punishment and His wrath will fall upon everyone who has broken His law who has not put their faith in Christ. But for now, I want you to understand that if you get sick, it's not because you have sinned. If you're struggling at work or your kids are struggling at school, it's not because you have sinned. That is not the God of the Bible. That is not His heart toward you.

What God does is use the Law to show us how to get to the foot of the cross. The Law leads us to faith. Exodus

14:31 tells us, "Israel saw the great power that the LORD used against the Egyptians, so the people feared the LORD, and they believed in the LORD and in his servant Moses."

God had just led His enslaved people out of Egypt and parted the Red Sea so that they could escape—and then closed the Red Sea back up on the Egyptians who were pursuing them. They witnessed God's fullness and His enormous power, and they were stunned. On the other side of the Red Sea, the Israelites were now safe and free. They were celebrating their deliverance and confessing their faith in the God who delivered them.

Within a few months, those same people who declared their faith in God were now bickering and murmuring against Him (Exodus 14:11). God saw the unbelief churning in their hearts, and He established what we know as the Ten Commandments.

The Ten Commandments begin with Exodus 20:2–3, "I am the LORD your God, who brought you out of the land of Egypt, out of the house of slavery. You shall have no other gods before me." God was asking the Israelites to trust Him—unlike Adam and Eve did—before He gave them the rules about what was right and what was wrong.

You and I are no different from Adam and Eve, and we are no different from the Israelites. We struggle with trusting God. When things are going the way we want, we can celebrate and praise God. But when life gets tough, trusting God becomes more difficult for us.

We live in a broken, fallen world. We're going to spend a lot more time in the valleys than we are on the mountaintops. This isn't because your life is messed up. It's because the world is messed up. We will spend most of our lives in the valley, and this is where our faith is vital. This is where we are to stand firm and worship God and seek Him. This is where we learn to passionately desire God's glory in our lives because we see what sin has done to us and those around us.

This is how things are supposed to work for us, but we tend to focus on the mountaintop experiences and the celebrations and wonder why we can't live in that place. God asks us to trust Him. Adam and Eve refused to, and the Israelites didn't fare much better.

"And the LORD said to Moses, 'How long will this people despise me? And how long will they not believe in me, in spite of all the signs that I have done among them?'" (Numbers 14:11). After the mountaintop experience of the parting of the Red Sea and their deliverance from Egypt, the Israelites had been trudging through a valley. They had gone from celebrating and worshiping God to despising Him, from having faith to not believing.

Likewise, you and I have moments of great belief and moments of not-so-great belief. Our trials should be sharpening and strengthening our faith—showing us God's glory and helping us to understand the Law leading to love and the Law leading to faith. Instead, we tend to falter at the first sign of difficulty and question how God could even be real if He allows things like this to happen to us.

And yet, when these trials, these valleys, come, we find ourselves on our knees, begging God to set things right. Any questions we had about His existence or why He allows bad things to happen to good people temporarily evaporate as we ask Him to help us. Our lives end up being a roller coaster between mountaintops and valleys when they could be a road.

Stuck Between the Law and the Cross

The Law is the road that leads us to the foot of the cross. I don't know about you, but when I'm on this road, sometimes I find myself hiding because I don't want to talk about my sin. I don't want to discuss it with other people, and I don't want to discuss it with God. I know that I have sinned against a holy and righteous God, and that it's because of my lack of faith, my lack of trust, my lack of discipline. I know all this—I just don't want to deal with it.

And if you're anything like me, you get stuck on this road between the Law and the foot of the cross, and you feel like you're standing in a moment of judgment. You feel like the spotlight is on you and God is getting ready to start throwing stones.

If this is your story, like it is mine, I want you to understand that there is a remedy. This gap between the Law leading to love, the Law leading to faith, and the Law leading to the foot of the cross is crucial for us to understand, and it's found in Romans 3:19–22:

> *Now we know that whatever the law says it speaks to those who are under the law, so that every mouth may be stopped, and the whole world may be held accountable to God. For by works of the law no human being will be justified in his sight, since through the law comes knowledge of sin. But now the righteousness of God has been manifested apart from the law, although the Law and the Prophets bear*

> *witness to it—the righteousness of God through faith in Jesus Christ for all who believe.*

Essentially, the Law is God telling us, "I know that you wanted the authority to determine what is right and what is wrong, but you can't have it because it's Mine." The Law, not our sinful hearts, is the authority, and it makes us aware of our sin.

But there is something other than the Law that will show us the glory and righteousness of God. The Law pointed us to what's right and what's wrong, but now there's something else that points us to what's right and wrong. What is this something else? It's the righteousness of God through faith in Jesus Christ.

The Law gave us an awareness of sin, but now something else has been established apart from the Law to give us righteousness before God, and that is faith. The Law leads us to faith. When God's Word begins to open this up, redemptive history becomes a reality for us.

The Law identifies our sin, our heart issue, and establishes that our road to the cross goes through love and faith. All too often, however, we get incorrectly bogged down in guilt over our sins, because we view the Law as punishment. We believe there's no way God could forgive us and love us. We feel like He must want to punish us, and so we feel judged.

But God lovingly and creatively put the Scriptures together to give us a road map to redemption. He created us, we sinned, and He established the Law to guide us to love and faith.

WORKBOOK

Chapter Four Questions

Question: What is your initial response when you hear the word *law*? What feelings does the topic of law bring up for you? Why do you think that is?

Action: Make a list of some of the moral laws you can find in the Torah and elsewhere in the Bible. For each law you find, write a sentence or two about how God uses that law to lead us to love, faith, and the foot of the cross.

____

____

____

____

____

____

____

____

____

____

____

____

Chapter Four Notes

CHAPTER FIVE

The Judges

by Brandon Weir

The fourth marker to help us in our understanding of Scripture is the judges. I owe much of the information and layout of this chapter to my good friend Brandon Weir.

When we think of judges, the images that come to mind for most of us are a robe and a gavel. While this isn't altogether untrue of the biblical judges, it misses a holistic view of the office of judges in the Bible.

The biblical interpretation of a judge was first and foremost a leader—more specifically, a leader of the Israelite people. These judges were empowered by God to lead the people in battle, politics, and spiritual matters. Not all the judges were spiritual leaders we would necessarily want to emulate, but they were endowed by God to save the people of Israel from the oppression they faced from rival nations around them. They were ordinary people raised up by God to do extraordinary things.

> *Then the LORD raised up judges, who saved them out of the hand of those who plundered them.*
>
> ***—Judges 2:16***

The judges and the battles they led seem unreal to us in our day and age. Their great feats seem like something you would see in a movie. We are drawn to stories and movies—in fact, superhero movies rake in millions of dollars a year—because we like to see the unreal accomplished.

I remember when my son was young, he was a superhero for Halloween. He was dressed up head to toe with the mask, the gloves, and even the shoes. The problem was, he was just young enough to be scared most of the night. He desperately wanted to accomplish the task of filling his candy bucket, but at any scary houses, he would immediately crawl up my leg—so I would have to pick him up in my arms and carry him to the front door to receive the candy he wanted so badly.

We see this same plot play out when judges accomplished God's will because they allowed themselves to be carried by God in order to lead the nation. These defining moments in Israel's history point us not to the judges, but instead to the powerful God who was carrying them to success.

The themes of the Israelites' story under the leadership of the judges are rebellion, despair, and deliverance against all odds. The book of Judges highlights what's referred to as the sin cycle of Israel. It's a loop we see in Scripture where Israel served the Lord, fell into sin (most commonly in the form of idolatry), became enslaved, and then cried out to the Lord in their slavery. Once they cried out to the Lord, God raised up a judge to deliver them.

It was a pattern that replicated itself often in the lives of the Israelite people; it also happens in ours. Sin is enticing and threatens to enslave us to itself, because we all find sin enticing, just like the Israelites. Without the saving grace of Jesus, we are destined to live in a place of shame, guilt, or apathy toward our sin. As was the case with the Israelite people, our only hope is the salvation of the Lord.

> *Whenever the LORD raised up judges for them, the LORD was with the judge, and he saved them from the hand of their enemies all the days of the judge. For the LORD was moved to pity by their groaning because of those who afflicted and oppressed them.*
>
> ***—Judges 2:18***

Raised Up

The Israelite people had their "fathers" of the faith: Abraham, Isaac, and Jacob. These men were seen as founders of the nation of Israel. Next followed Joseph, who brought his family into the land of Egypt. They prospered there for many years but were eventually taken into slavery by the Egyptian people. These were years where it seemed as if the people of Israel had lost their place as the chosen people of God. But then Moses led the people out of slavery and into the land that was promised to them as God's people.

Along the way, Moses gave the people the Law, which

acted as a guide for how the people of God were to live. The Law was meant to guide the people toward love and faith, but who was going to administer the Law and hold the people accountable? The thing about accountability is that no one really likes being held accountable all the time.

I remember a road trip during which I learned firsthand that I did not appreciate being held accountable for everything. My daughter was just old enough to understand laws and be able to read street signs, so her mother thought it would be fun to teach her about speed limit signs. This became an issue for me because I wasn't paying as close attention to the signs as my daughter was in her new hobby. My daughter would see a sign, call out the speed, look at the speedometer from the back seat, and announce that I was a lawbreaker.

I would recognize my fault, but moments later, I would realize I wasn't making the time I wanted—so I would speed up again. She would once again broadcast my shortcomings. The game ultimately ended when I made the decision to use a notecard to cover my speedometer so no one would know how fast I was going. In short, I eliminated my accountability.

God knew people needed accountability. Therefore, He raised up great leaders to help lead people to God. These great leaders understood the Law was for accountability, so they led from that platform. Moses eventually passed the torch of leadership to Joshua, and it was Joshua's call to lead them into the Promised Land.

Moses entrusted leadership of the people to Joshua, in whom he had invested, showing him what leadership should look like. In losing Moses and then Joshua, the

Israelites lost their spiritual accountability. Their time spent living in a land without God was just as full of despair as their time as slaves in Egypt.

When we pick up their journey in the book of Judges, the people finally had a land to call their own, but they did not have a leader. It seemed at first to be working out; they finally had the land they had longed for. They had achieved earthly success, but they ended up failing spiritually. This type of success is a trapping in our world. Earthly success coupled with failure in the eyes of God begins early in Judges.

In Judges 1:1, the people asked after Joshua's death who would go up and fight against the Canaanites for them. It's a picture of unity, but it also shows a lack of leadership among their ranks. The Canaanites were there and needed to be reckoned with. They did not know where to turn, so they inquired of God. Trusting in God would work as long as they stayed faithful to Him, but as we will see, they did not. They quickly turned toward foreign gods and began to live like the foreign nations around them. When Joshua died, the people floundered and did not follow God.

In the beginning of Judges, the people were united: "After the death of Joshua, the people of Israel inquired of the LORD, 'Who shall go up first for us against the Canaanites, to fight against them?'" (Judges 1:1). But subsequently, the people drifted toward disobedience. Instead of removing the foreign people and their foreign gods from their land, they allowed these people to stay and eventually gave into these influences. As a result, God raised up judges to lead the people back to Him.

What does it mean to be raised up? For the judges, it was to serve God's people, to help pull them out of despair. For us, it's to live out the calling God has in front of us. It's an incredible blessing to be obedient to this calling and to experience the life God intends for us to have, but it is robbed from us by sin and believing the false promises of this world. The world tells us that to be whole, we must fill ourselves with as much as possible of what the world has to offer. But God tells us true fulfillment is found in the path of self-denial and service to the King.

How can a person serve a king joyfully and with their whole will? First, they must believe the king is worthy of serving and that the king is a good king.

The Judges and the Law

God gave people the Law to teach them how to know and follow Him. It helps show what a people who follow God looks like. The Law was overseen by judges after the people of Israel failed to obey God. These judges were seen as leaders of the people, both physically and spiritually. They led the people into battle and into obeying God.

We learned in Chapter Four that the Law is meant to lead people into a place of love and faith in God. The judges were meant to be a physical representation of this. They were to guide the people toward God and keep them in line with the great calling God had placed on their lives.

It doesn't matter where we pick up with the Scriptures; all roads lead back to a relationship with God. The astounding thing about Scripture is, all of it points toward the heart of a Father who wants to be in relationship with

His children. Many times, we can lose sight of this because we're enamored of the stories or trying to follow the rules in the Bible. All of the Bible is God revealing Himself to people and calling them into relationship because He loves them.

Later, God raised up the perfect Judge—Jesus. In Him we find the true road to a relationship with God and a Savior who was willing to lay down His life for us. Jesus would perfectly follow the Law in all the ways we're unable to.

> *For our sake he made him to be sin who knew no sin, so that in him we might become the righteousness of God.*
>
> ***—2 Corinthians 5:21***

A Good Judge or a Bad Judge

> *And what more shall I say? For time would fail me to tell of Gideon, Barak, Samson, Jephthah, of David and Samuel and the prophets—who through faith conquered kingdoms, enforced justice, obtained promises, stopped the mouths of lions, quenched the power of fire, escaped the edge of the sword, were made strong out of weakness, became mighty in war, put foreign armies to flight.*
>
> ***—Hebrews 11:32–34***

The judges were a display of God's goodness and grace toward His people. When the Israelites despaired and had nowhere else to turn, God raised one up in their midst to show them the way. As with the kings later on, the judges were a fallible bandage on a gaping wound, which was the disobedience of the people.

The judges' stories are some of the most remarkable in all of Scripture: Samson killing a thousand men with the jawbone of a donkey, the tent peg crushing a man's skull when Deborah was a judge, or Ehud stabbing a large man with his left hand. While the victories were incredible, it's the failure of many of the judges and of the people that stands out to us the most. The judges were not a perfect embodiment of the Law; they were simply called to oversee it. They failed tremendously throughout their time. Whether it was Samson and his sexual sin, or Gideon and his inability to trust in God, they—like the people they led—all struggled to obey God's commands. All the judges, much like us, had triumphs and failures.

So, how do we reconcile the failures with their placement in the Hebrews 11 "hall of faith"? I learned to reconcile failure and faith early in my spiritual journey. I learned not to put anyone other than Christ on a pedestal, because even the faithful have failures.

My high school soccer coach was also a mentor of mine who discipled me constantly. He spent hours and hours investing in my spiritual formation. He would meet with me before school for Bible studies and Scripture memorization, completely investing in my growth and decision making. I viewed my coach as someone who could have been listed in Hebrews chapter 11's hall of faith; he was a spiritual giant to me.

A few years after high school, I found out he was unfaithful to his wife, and I heard so many conversations questioning his integrity. I myself wrestled with the question of *"how?"* What I grew to realize was that I had seen his good, and I had received his good, so I knew his faith was real. I reconciled his failure with his faith by recognizing he was never meant to be on a pedestal. Instead, he was simply pointing me to the one on the pedestal, who is Christ.

Using that same logic, the book of Judges is quick to point out that the acts of deliverance the judges brought about were due to the empowerment of the Holy Spirit, not their perfection or innate strength. The Spirit of God was the one to save the people.

The judges were not role models, and they were not heroes. They were chosen servants of God to carry out His purposes. Jesus is the only Hero.

We have to be careful of the people we put on pedestals, being cautious to not count them as our saviors. People are people, and every person has their own strengths and weaknesses. If we hold them to unattainable standards, they will surely fail, and we will surely be disappointed. Our world loves to watch people stumble and fall, especially if it's someone of stature. Maybe part of our frustration within the church today is a result of elevating leaders and pastors to an unhealthy degree. Jesus is the only one worthy of being lifted up in our lives.

Through it all, one of the most inspiring parts of the judges is that they were flawed human beings whom God used to do incredible things. This should be encouraging to us because we are flawed and often struggling with our own sin. Yet, God can use flawed, struggling people to do great works for His kingdom.

How Do We Break Out of our Sin Cycle?

The people of Israel were caught in a sin cycle, which ultimately led them to their downfall. They struggled to remain faithful to God and were led astray by the temptations of this world. Israel had experienced the deliverance of God, but still, they could not remain faithful. They were the chosen nation of God, and they failed miserably. How can we hope to succeed where they failed?

We feel the weight of the sin cycle in our own lives. We feel the heavy weight of returning to things we know will only leave us empty and feeling far from God. How do we break free from the sin cycle in our lives? The apostle Paul, the "super-Christian" himself, talked about his own struggle to break out of the sin that so easily entangles him. In Romans 7:15, he wrote, "For I do not understand my own actions. For I do not do what I want, but I do the very thing I hate." Paul found himself doing the very things he hated. His sin seemed to take on a life of its own, and while he wanted to do right, he said he did not have the ability to do it. Imagine Paul being unable to say no to sin. What hope could there possibly be for us?

But there is hope, because the ability to live for God is not something found within ourselves; it's found in the one who was raised up on a cross for our sins. Paul saw Jesus as his deliverer from this "body of death" (Romans 6:25). It's as Peter told us, "He himself bore our sins in his body on the tree, that we might die to sin and live to righteousness. By his wounds you have been healed" (1 Peter 1:24).

Jesus bore our sins on the cross. Think about how

excruciating that must have been. Paul's own sin seemed to overwhelm him. Yet, Jesus bore the sins of the world in His body on the cross. He did this so that we might be declared righteous while trying to live a righteous life. The only way we are going to live for righteousness is found in Jesus. We cannot be good enough to get to God. God's promises don't come to us because of our goodness, but because He has promised them, and we trust in Him.

The judges were there to remind the people that humans fail and ultimately, we would need greater leadership than any regular person could offer. Only God can offer the kind of love and leadership that will truly change the hearts of people. The Israelites did not heed this warning and instead began looking for a king: "In those days there was no king in Israel. Everyone did what was right in his own eyes" (Judges 21:25).

They believed a king would save them. We put our belief in all sorts of things to save us, but there is only one true Judge who has the ability and desire to erase our sins and failures. Like I carried my young son in his superhero costume through the hard moments on that Halloween night, God is there to carry us through the hard parts of life.

WORKBOOK

Chapter Five Questions

Question: How do you see the pattern of the Israelites reflected in your own life (falling into sin, becoming enslaved, and crying out to the Lord)? How does God meet you in that cycle?

____

____

____

____

____

____

____

____

____

____

____

Action: Pick a judge in the Bible to study. Write about who they were, what they did, and what God called them to do. List their mistakes and their successes and how God used them. How does their example influence your perspective on God's ability to use you for His purposes?

____

____

____

____

____

____

____

____

____

____

____

____

Chapter Five Notes

CHAPTER SIX

The Kings

The fifth marker that will help us to navigate through Scripture is the kings. Before we start the transition and history of the kings, it is important we understand that we all have kings in our lives.

I grew up in the '80s and spent most of my weekends at a place called Skateland in Tulsa, Oklahoma. Outside of skating on four wheels and listening to the best music ever made, there were also games such as limbo, the big dice game, and of course races. Skateland had a particular game called "King of the Hill."

This last one was a simple game. You would race with eight kids to the opposite side of the rink, where there was a circle only big enough for four kids, which meant the first four to the circle who could stay in the circle would go on to the last round. In the last round, those four would race to the other side, where the circle was now only big enough for one skater—who would become the "King of the Hill."

My sister, who was older, wiser, and faster, was a dominant force in this particular game. She would win virtually every time and gloat to me, saying, "I'm the King of the Hill, I'm the King of the Hill!" One day during her gloating, I stopped her quickly by saying, "You are not the King—Randall Rusher is the real King of Skateland." Randall was older and cooler than her. He had spiked hair and a popped collar, and everyone wanted to be him.

At some point in that same day, I remember admiring the King of Skateland when it hit me: I had never seen him skate. I had never even seen him in roller skates. Why did I think he was King of Skateland when he hadn't ever skated?

The truth is, most of the kings in our lives are self-proclaimed without having earned that spot. This is the same truth we see play out in the Bible during the period of the kings. They never earned the title of king; it was given to them. As we study the kings, we cannot ignore that we give away kingship to things in our lives that have never earned the right to be king over us.

The period of the kings lasted for about five hundred years and included around fifty kings. The kings were part of an overarching history, and each king had a story within that history. However, the lesson learned from each king's story comes back to the same theme.

But first, how did Israel transition from being ruled by judges to being ruled by a king? The people of Israel no longer wanted judges, so they approached the prophet Samuel and asked him to appoint a king:

> *Then all the elders of Israel gathered together and came to Samuel at Ramah and said to him, "Behold, you are old and your sons do not walk in your ways. Now appoint for us a king to judge us like all the nations." But the thing displeased Samuel when they said, "Give us a king to judge us." And Samuel prayed to the LORD.*
>
> ***—1 Samuel 8:4–6***

As a result, in 1050 B.C., God gave Israel their first king, a man named Saul. The second king of Israel was David, who was known for being a man after God's own heart (1 Samuel 13:14), and the third king was David's son Solomon, who was known for his wisdom (1 Kings 3). And yet, the first three kings failed to be the guides and examples the Israelites were hoping the kings would be.

In 930 B.C., after Solomon's death, a monumental event took place.[14] There were twelve tribes in Israel, ten of which lived in the northern part of the country while two tribes lived in the south. When Rehoboam, Solomon's son, became the fourth king of Israel, the ten northern tribes sent representatives to speak with him and ask him to lower taxes (1 Kings 12).

Rehoboam refused, and the ten northern tribes became angry and decided to appoint their own king and set up their own kingdom. Two tribes remained loyal to Rehoboam—the tribes of Judah and Benjamin. The ten tribes in the northern part of the country became known as the Northern Kingdom, or Israel, and the two tribes in the southern part of the country became known as the Southern Kingdom, or Judah.

The Story of King Asa

Now that you have the history, we're going to skip ahead in the chronology of the kings to Asa, the third king of Judah, as he is the king who highlights our lesson—a lesson common to all of the kings. Let's take a look at 2 Chronicles 16:1, "In the thirty-sixth year of the reign of Asa, Baasha king of Israel went up against Judah and built Ramah, that he might permit no one to go out or come in to Asa king of Judah."

To clarify, the story of King Asa occurred in the middle of a war between Judah (the Southern Kingdom) and Israel (the Northern Kingdom). The king of Israel decided he was going to build an enormous wall so no one could come in or out of Judah. He was trying to starve Judah into giving up and giving him control of their kingdom. Asa concluded there was no way the two tribes of Judah could defeat the ten tribes of Israel. They were completely outnumbered. So, he devised a plan:

> *Then Asa took silver and gold from the treasures of the house of the LORD and the king's house and sent them to Ben-hadad king of Syria, who lived in Damascus, saying, "There is a covenant between me and you, as there was between my father and your father. Behold, I am sending to you silver and gold. Go, break your covenant with Baasha king of Israel, that he may withdraw from me."*
>
> ***—2 Chronicles 16:2–3***

Asa stole silver and gold from the temple treasury and used it to enlist the aid of a foreign king. That was a pretty nice payment for Ben-hadad, and he did what Asa asked:

> *And Ben-hadad listened to King Asa and sent the commanders of his armies against the cities of Israel, and they conquered Ijon, Dan, Abel-maim, and all the store cities of Naphtali. And when Baasha heard of it, he stopped building Ramah and let his work cease. Then King Asa took all Judah, and they carried away the stones of Ramah and its timber, with which Baasha had been building, and with them he built Geba and Mizpah.*
>
> ***—2 Chronicles 16:4–6***

The Syrian armies started attacking Israel from the opposite side. All of Israel's fighting men were at the border of Judah, working to build the city of Ramah. They had no choice but to abandon construction and rush off to defend their territory from the Syrians. Meanwhile, the people of Judah dismantled Ramah and used the materials to build two cities of their own.

It was a perfect scenario for Asa. Syria was attacking Israel, so Israel was off his back, and he was able to add two new cities to his kingdom. He must've been pretty proud of himself. Unfortunately, Asa fell into the same trap that Adam and Eve fell into—and the same trap that the judges fell into. They wanted everything to be controlled by their own hands.

Fifty different kings over five hundred years of history also fell into this same trap, repeatedly choosing to take matters into their own hands instead of trusting God. And what's ironic is, even though we know their histories, those stories end up becoming our stories. Asa's story is no different from ours.

A Lesson from King Asa

Now we come to the lesson of Asa's story—and for that matter, the lesson of all the kings' stories. Second Chronicles 16:7 tells us, "At that time Hanani the seer came to Asa king of Judah and said to him, 'Because you relied on the king of Syria, and did not rely on the LORD your God, the army of the king of Syria has escaped you.'"

History shows us that Syria continued to grow bigger and bigger and ultimately overthrew Israel. Judah would eventually be overthrown by the Babylonians. All twelve tribes would go through extremely dark and difficult times because Asa allowed the king of Syria to "escape" him, which meant Asa had given him power. Through Asa's actions, Syria gained money, territory, and people, and they continued to conquer and expand. Syria ultimately wanted all of Israel—so they came and took it.

The lesson here is, when the time came, Asa did not rely on or trust God. Adam and Eve did not rely on or trust God. Otherwise, they wouldn't have eaten the fruit. The judges did not rely on or trust God. Otherwise, those seven sin cycles wouldn't have taken place. The kings did not rely on or trust God. Otherwise, they and their kingdoms would not have crumbled over five hundred years of history.

You and I are no different. We continually struggle to rely on and trust God. Even though we know He is our Creator and our King, we still try to take matters into our own hands. When things in our lives begin to crumble, we try to fix it ourselves instead of turning to God and relying on Him. And when we do this, we're telling our holy and righteous God who loves us and wants to protect us and take care of us that He isn't good enough to do those things. That's what we're communicating with our hearts and with our lives.

Asa was not pleased with what Hanani the seer said to him. I can imagine him protesting that he used God's money from the temple treasury to pay off the king of Syria—didn't that count as relying on God?

But Hanani had more to say: "Were not the Ethiopians and the Libyans a huge army with very many chariots and horsemen? Yet because you relied on the LORD, he gave them into your hand" (2 Chronicles 16:8). Hanani reminded Asa that he had faced bigger trials than this and that when he had trusted God, God provided for him. So why didn't he trust God this time?

Hanani continued: "For the eyes of the LORD run to and fro throughout the whole earth, to give strong support to those whose heart is blameless toward him. You have done foolishly in this, for from now on you will have wars" (2 Chronicles 16:9).

The heart has been a common theme for us, and it's a common theme throughout Scripture as well. The issue here was Asa's heart. Every time we take matters into our own hands instead of relying on God and trusting Him, we are acting foolishly, just like Asa did.

When we go through trials, it's our nature to become bitter and angry and to allow these emotions to consume us. That is sin. And when we let sin fester by choosing to deal with our trials our way, we stay at war internally all the days of our lives because we don't rely on God to forgive us and heal us.

Asa's lesson applies to any situation we might find ourselves in. It's a failure to trust God. It's the failure to rely on God. And this hurts and stifles our walk with Him. Our lack of reliance on God creates in us an ability to sin and not be remorseful. It leads us to be people who not only tolerate sin but condone it as well. We should hate sin—especially our own.

After listening to Hanani and taking out his anger on him and the people (2 Chronicles 16:10), Asa spent the next two years of his life at war with everyone and everything, but mostly with himself. Three years after his disastrous decision involving the king of Syria, Asa developed a foot disease (2 Chronicles 16:12). He died two years later (2 Chronicles 16:13).

What Is the King in Your Life?

Asa didn't live much longer after he chose to take matters into his own hands instead of relying on God, and as Hanani prophesied, the remainder of his life was spent at war. I can't help wondering why he would choose to spend the last few years of his life in misery. Why didn't he repent before God and admit his sin? He never reached that point of repentance. My fear is that some of us would be content to remain at war with ourselves when all we really need to do is acknowledge our holy and sovereign God and choose to trust Him with every ounce of our being.

Let me give you a paraphrase of Isaiah 6:1: in the year that King Uzziah died, the glory of the Lord filled the temple. I've read that scripture numerous times, but it didn't come to life for me until I started putting all of this together. When we accept Jesus as our Lord and Savior by accepting what He did for us on the cross, His Holy Spirit takes up residence inside of us. First Corinthians 3:16 says, "Do you not know that you are God's temple and that God's Spirit dwells in you?"

However, each one of us has a king in our lives who needs to die in order for God to truly fill us. The reason we do not fall on our knees and passionately seek God in prayer through the good and the bad in our lives is that we have decided to turn to our other kings and rely on them to see us through whatever we are struggling with.

Jesus tells us, "Come to me, all who labor and are heavy laden, and I will give you rest" (Matthew 11:28), but instead, we turn to our addictions, our strongholds. We turn to the kings we have created. And even though I'm referring to them as kings, let's be honest: they're sin. There is habitual sin that exists in each and every one of us, and until we learn to kill it and destroy it, the glory of the Lord cannot fully fill us for His purposes. We won't be able to see all of His goodness because we are stuck in our self-reliance and we can only see the mess that's in front of us.

We are tethered to the sin of this world, and we act like we don't care. As people who want to pursue Jesus passionately, we need to understand that the kings in our life have to die so we can know Christ more fully. Maybe your king is anger. It looms over you, and you just can't get away from it. That is the sin that controls you, the king that dominates you. Maybe your king is loneliness or depression. You allow it to lord over you, and you try to fix it on your own instead of seeking God for peace and restoration. Your king might be a particular addiction. Every time something starts to crunch against you, you run to that vice. You know how destructive it's been in your life, and you've seen what it's done to your family, but you continue to let that king remain on its throne.

The list of possible kings is nearly endless. My question for you is this: now that you understand the history of the kings, a story of one of the kings, and the overall lesson we can learn from the kings about their failure to rely on God, what will you do? What king do you need to dethrone in your life so the glory of God can fill you? What habitual sin, what stumbling block, is preventing you from being the man or woman of God you want to be?

I found out why Randall Rusher was never skating: he did not know how! Never elevate other people, relationships, addictions, or you yourself to the status of king in your life. We must dethrone our small kings so the true King reigns!

WORKBOOK

Chapter Six Questions

Question: In what area of your life are you communicating through your actions that you don't trust God? How are you attempting to take matters into your own hands?

____

____

____

____

____

____

____

____

____

____

____

____

Action: Determine the king in your heart that needs to be dethroned so God's Spirit can fill you and rule your life. When you identify it, spend time in prayer and allow God to take His rightful place as King in your life.

Chapter Six Notes

CHAPTER SEVEN

The Prophets

The sixth marker that will help us to navigate through Scripture is the prophets. In Numbers 12:6, God was speaking with Moses, Aaron, and Miriam: "And he said, 'Hear my words: If there is a prophet among you, I the LORD make myself known to him in a vision; I speak with him in a dream.'" A prophet is someone to whom God speaks or gives a vision and who then speaks and acts accordingly. They hear from God, and then they speak or enact what He has told them.

There are many prophets throughout Scripture, so why have I chosen to include them at this point in the series of markers, after the kings? Moses and Noah would certainly be considered prophets, as they both heard from God and acted. The same is true of Jacob, Joseph, and Deborah, who was one of the judges. Saul, the first king of Israel, also prophesied (1 Samuel 10). So why does the marker of the prophets only appear in the structure now?

The answer is straightforward: the placement of the marker of the prophets reflects the order of the books in the Bible. There are seventeen books that focus on the prophets, and they come between the books focusing on the kings and the books of the New Testament. Five of these books of the prophets (Isaiah, Jeremiah, Lamentations, Ezekiel, and Daniel) are known as the major prophets, and the other twelve are known as the minor prophets. The main distinction between the major prophets and the minor prophets is simply that the major prophets wrote longer books.

There are thousands of prophecies in Scripture, and many have already been fulfilled. Typically, there is a gap of time between when a prophecy is spoken and when it is fulfilled. Sometimes that gap of time is a few days or months, and sometimes it's years or even centuries. Many of the people who heard the prophecy spoken didn't see it come to pass. For example, the prophets spoke about Jesus in great detail—His birth, His birthplace, His life, His betrayal, His death, His burial, His resurrection—centuries before He was born. The people who originally heard these prophecies about Jesus never saw them fulfilled.

The prophets spoke about the present, but most of the time, they spoke about the future. That's why the prophets had two main functions. Their first function was to serve as a preacher. They heard from God, and they told the people what He said. Their second function was to serve as a predictor. God gave them a vision of what was going to happen in the future, and they shared it with the people. They spoke of what was to come.

Now that we see where the prophets fit among the nine markers, it's also important to understand how God used the prophets. Each one was used uniquely for their time, place, and audience. Let's take a closer look at one prophet to understand the radical ways God used *prophets* in general to connect His *people* back to His *purpose*.

Ezekiel: God's Use of Prophets

The prophet we will zoom in on is Ezekiel, who was one of the major prophets. Ezekiel lived around 597 B.C.[15] We have previously discussed how everything started to collapse for the kings around 930 B.C., when Solomon died and was succeeded by his son Rehoboam.[16] Due to Rehoboam's refusal to reduce taxes, the kingdom split into the northern kingdom of Israel, which was made up of ten tribes, and the southern kingdom of Judah, which was made up of two tribes.[17]

Over the next 350 years, both kingdoms crumbled. Israel was ultimately taken into captivity and exiled by the Assyrians, Judah was also taken into captivity and exile by the Babylonians. As a result, the city of Jerusalem was in ruins. In fact, in the book of Nehemiah, Nehemiah returned from exile in Babylon to assess the damage to the city and see what was needed to restore it.

Ezekiel came on the scene in 597 B.C.[18] At this point, the Babylonians had already conquered Judah, where Ezekiel was from, and Ezekiel had been exiled to Babylon. Ezekiel 1:1 tells us, "In the *thirtieth* year, in the fourth month, on the fifth day of the month, as I was among the exiles by the Chebar canal, the heavens were opened, and I saw visions of God" (emphasis mine).

Ezekiel's vision took place in his thirtieth year, which is significant. Why wait until Ezekiel was thirty? In

Numbers 4, we see that priestly service for men belonging to the tribe of Levi began at age thirty. Jesus didn't start His public ministry until He was thirty years old (Luke 3:23). He waited until He was the proper age for beginning priestly service in accordance with that law. Ezekiel was establishing here that he had the authority to be a priest.

Continuing in that verse, Ezekiel said that he "saw visions of God." The book of Revelation, for example, is a single vision from God to John the apostle. Ezekiel, on the other hand, had multiple visions. He received his call to be a prophet in Ezekiel 2:1–3:

> *And he said to me, "Son of man, stand on your feet, and I will speak with you." And as he spoke to me, the Spirit entered into me and set me on my feet, and I heard him speaking to me. And he said to me, "Son of man, I send you to the people of Israel, to nations of rebels, who have rebelled against me. They and their fathers have transgressed against me to this very day."*

As we've previously discussed, Israel at this point was divided into two main groups: the people of Israel, who were now in Syria, and the people of Judah, who were now in Babylon. There was also a remnant, or those who remained, in Jerusalem. Even though His people had been scattered in exile, God still saw them as His people.

Seventy-two times in the book of Ezekiel, God said, "Know that I am the LORD" (ESV).[19] God created us for His glory, but that was broken by sin. He established Himself as our God through the Law, the judges, and the kings.

And yet, God's people continued to rebel and reject Him. This rejection started in the garden of Eden, and it kept on going.

And so, Ezekiel's prophetic assignments began. God instructed him to set up an elaborate scene to illustrate to the exiles what was happening in Jerusalem:

> *And you, son of man, take a brick and lay it before you, and engrave on it a city, even Jerusalem. And put siegeworks against it, and build a siege wall against it, and cast up a mound against it. Set camps also against it, and plant battering rams against it all around. And you, take an iron griddle, and place it as an iron wall between you and the city; and set your face toward it, and let it be in a state of siege, and press the siege against it. This is a sign for the house of Israel.*
>
> ***—Ezekiel 4:1–3***

Ezekiel recreated Jerusalem, only to lay siege to it and destroy it. It was intended as a representation of what the people's sin had done to their homeland. Because of their sin, they were losing what God had promised them as Babylon continued to conquer Jerusalem. But it didn't stop there. God had another object lesson for Ezekiel to act out:

> *And you, O son of man, take a sharp sword. Use it as a barber's razor and pass it over your head and your beard. Then take balances for weighing and divide the hair. A third part you shall burn in the fire in the midst of the city, when the days of the siege are completed. And a third part you shall take and strike with the sword all around the city. And a third part you shall scatter to the wind, and I will unsheathe*

> *the sword after them. And you shall take from these a small number and bind them in the skirts of your robe. And of these again you shall take some and cast them into the midst of the fire and burn them in the fire. From there a fire will come out into all the house of Israel. Thus says the Lord GOD: This is Jerusalem. I have set her in the center of the nations, with countries all around her.*
>
> ***—Ezekiel 5:1–5***

God then explained what Ezekiel's actions with his freshly shaven hair meant:

> *A third part of you shall die of pestilence and be consumed with famine in your midst; a third part shall fall by the sword all around you; and a third part I will scatter to all the winds and will unsheathe the sword after them.*
>
> ***—Ezekiel 5:12***

Such would be the fate of the people who remained in Jerusalem (Ezekiel 5:5).

These were only two of numerous prophetic actions God asked Ezekiel to undertake to show the exiles in Babylon what was happening in Jerusalem and why it was happening. As mentioned earlier in the chapter, Ezekiel also had multiple visions. Ezekiel 8 describes one of these visions, in which God transported Ezekiel to the temple in Jerusalem:

> *And he brought me to the entrance of the court, and when I looked, behold, there was a hole in the wall. Then he said to me, "Son of man, dig in the wall." So I dug in the wall, and behold, there was an entrance. And he said to me, "Go in, and see the vile abominations that they are committing*

> *here." So I went in and saw. And there, engraved on the wall all around, was every form of creeping things and loathsome beasts, and all the idols of the house of Israel. ... Then he said to me, "Have you seen this, O son of man? Is it too light a thing for the house of Judah to commit the abominations that they commit here, that they should fill the land with violence and provoke me still further to anger? Behold, they put the branch to their nose. Therefore I will act in wrath. My eye will not spare, nor will I have pity. And though they cry in my ears with a loud voice, I will not hear them."*
>
> ***—Ezekiel 8:7–10, 17–18***

The people were far from God because they had created all of those other gods for themselves. They no longer worshiped Him as the one, true, sovereign God. God made it clear to Ezekiel that Ezekiel needed to be faithful to Him and follow His instructions. And as we can see from his book, Ezekiel obeyed. No matter how bizarre the prophetic action or how unsettling the vision, Ezekiel did everything God asked him to do.

Ezekiel: The Central Message of All Prophets

This brings us to Ezekiel's message, which is also the central message of all the prophets. Remember, when the prophets spoke, there was typically a gap before what they had prophesied was fulfilled. The prophets spoke to the present, and they also spoke to the future. This means that what they had to say is still relevant to us today.

Ezekiel shared his message in Ezekiel 37:15–19:

> *The word of the LORD came to me: "Son of man, take a stick and write on it, 'For Judah, and the people of Israel*

> *associated with him'; then take another stick and write on it, 'For Joseph (the stick of Ephraim) and all the house of Israel associated with him.' And join them one to another into one stick, that they may become one in your hand. And when your people say to you, 'Will you not tell us what you mean by these?' say to them, Thus says the Lord GOD: Behold, I am about to take the stick of Joseph (that is in the hand of Ephraim) and the tribes of Israel associated with him. And I will join with it the stick of Judah, and make them one stick, that they may be one in my hand."*

It sounds simple enough, but remember the history that had taken place before all of this. There had been 350 years of division and hatred between the kingdoms of Israel and Judah. It was a dark and terrible time in the history of God's people. When Ezekiel told the people that Israel and Judah were going to be united again, it almost seemed like satire. It would've been difficult for the people to take him seriously.

But there is a key, pivotal phrase at the end of these verses. It is the central theme God wanted us and the people at that time to hear through all of the prophets: "…that they may be one in my hand" (Ezekiel 37:19). God was saying, if His people come back to Him and know He is God, He will restore them.

I had the privilege of marrying my high school sweetheart, and we have been together for over three decades. Over the years, we have learned how to love each other more every day. For the most part, she can finish my thoughts and knows what I'm going to do before I do it—especially at the end of a heated discussion.

In the area of conflict, I have always struggled with simply saying, "I'm sorry." As simple as those words are, they just don't roll off my tongue very easily. After all, words are words, and I believe in actions—or at least, that's what I say to make myself feel better. So, when I've pushed the envelope too far, I will find the right time, slide up next to my bride, and take her hand. She then gives me a little side-eye and a smirk and says, "Do you have anything you want to say?"

And I reply, "No, do you?"

She giggles and says, "I assume that's your apology?"

Then I nod, and all is restored. It's not the traditional approach, but it's ours, and it works. This reminds me of the phrase Ezekiel recorded, "one in my hand." When we hold hands with someone, both are at peace.

But there's still more to Ezekiel's message—and to the message of all the prophets. God continued:

> *When the sticks on which you write are in your hand before their eyes, then say to them, Thus says the Lord GOD: Behold, I will take the people of Israel from the nations among which they have gone, and will gather them from all around, and bring them to their own land. And I will make them one nation in the land, on the mountains of Israel.*
>
> ***—Ezekiel 37:20–22***

Reconciliation is the second part of this, and it's just as crucial as the first part, restoration. God will restore us and reconcile us to Himself if only we will return to Him. This is the central theme of the prophets.

It gets even better, though. God continued in the second half of verse 22: "And one king shall be king over them all, and they shall be no longer two nations, and no longer divided into two kingdoms." This would've sounded like absolute insanity to the people. The people had asked God for a king (1 Samuel 8:4), and then they decided they didn't want a king. They wanted two kings, and so the nation divided (1 Kings 12). Factions and divisions then continued to build within the divided kingdoms. And now, God was telling the people they would once again be a united nation with one king.

God created us for His glory, and sin broke us, but through the prophets, He tells us that He has the ability to restore us and reconcile us to Himself. How is He going to do that? He is going to give us a King. That is the third and final part of Ezekiel's message and the message of all the prophets.

As we have seen in our journey through Scripture, however, God's people have a pattern of rejecting Him. Adam and Eve rejected Him in the garden of Eden, and His people went on to reject the Law, the judges, and the kings. Through all the rejection, we still see God's heart for the world and hear the theme of the prophets coming out in Ezekiel 37:23:

> *They shall not defile themselves anymore with their idols and their detestable things, or with any of their transgressions. But I will save them from all the backslidings in which they have sinned, and will cleanse them; and they shall be my people, and I will be their God.*

The word translated as "backslidings" is the Hebrew word for *dwellings*.[20] God was promising to save His people, which is also part of the central theme of the prophets, and He promised to save them in their current state. The people hearing Ezekiel's message were Israelites living in exile in Babylon who were unable to live according to the regulations in the Law, making them dirty and defiled.[21] And yet, God was willing to meet them in this current state, their dwelling, and save them.

God will restore us, He will reconcile us to Himself, and He will save us. That is the central theme of the prophets.

Let's take a closer look at the end of verse 23: "…[I] will cleanse them; and they shall be my people, and I will be their God." This must have been incredible for Ezekiel to hear, especially after all of his unusual prophetic assignments. And it's just as incredible for us to hear today.

We still live under the curse of sin, and there are things in our lives that are shattered and need to be restored. Even as Christians, our faith and our hope get broken at times, and we don't always know how to handle it. We run around asking the world, instead of going to Scripture and God to let Him help us. Our faith and our hope sometimes need to be restored because we live in a fallen, broken world, and the only time our faith and our hope can be restored is when we are in God's hands. It's a central theme.

In verse 23, God promises to cleanse us and make us His people. In essence, God was saying that His people will trust Him. They will trust Him, and He will be their God, their King, their Savior, and their restorer. As we have discussed previously, the central theme of Scripture overall is about the heart. This does not change with the prophets. The prophets are likewise concerned about the heart of humanity. As long as the human heart is away from God, it's broken, but when it's in God's hands, it can be made whole.

Restoration

What is broken and in need of restoration in your life and in your heart? In the previous chapter, I asked you to think about what king in your life needs to die, what consuming or habitual sin you need to deal with, in order for the glory of God to fill you. This is the second step in that process. First, we need to identify the king that needs to die, and once that king dies, we need to be restored.

How do we restore ourselves? We don't. We turn our eyes back to Him and His glory because that's where restoration is found—in Him. We are in desperate need of restoration, and God is the only one who can do it. He is a God who restores, reconciles, saves, and desires to be our God. That was the message of Ezekiel and the rest of the prophets to God's people then. And if we listen, we find it is the same message for us today.

WORKBOOK

Chapter Seven Questions

Question: In what area of your life are you in need of God's restoration and reconciliation? How can you demonstrate your trust in God to allow Him to bring that change and healing into your life?

Action: Have you fully accepted that you are God's and allowed Him to make you His? If you are still hesitating or unsure of your stance before God, spend some time writing out what prohibits you from turning your eyes to God and committing your life and heart to Him.

____

____

____

____

____

____

____

____

____

____

____

____

Chapter Seven Notes

CHAPTER EIGHT

Jesus

The seventh marker that will help us to navigate through Scripture is Jesus. All of Scripture points to Him.

When I was growing up, my dad fixed everything. If something broke, it didn't matter what it was; he would fix it. He had the ability to take in hand something that was completely broken and completely restore it. From cars to kites, he could literally fix anything.

What my father could do with material stuff, Jesus does with our soul. He restores our souls back to their original purpose. Jesus doesn't just fix us for a moment. He truly reconciles broken people to make them a restored people. Let's take a look at His kingship and what it is going to bring.

God promised David that "your house and your kingdom shall be made sure forever before me. Your throne shall be established forever" (2 Samuel 7:16). David's son Solomon succeeded him on the throne of Israel, and Solomon was followed by his son Rehoboam. But then, the kingdom of Israel split into the northern kingdom of Israel and the southern kingdom of Judah, with the throne of David remaining in Judah.

Jesus' genealogies are recorded in Matthew 1 and Luke 3. In Matthew 1, Joseph's lineage is listed as coming from David and his son Solomon. In Luke, Mary's lineage is listed as coming from David and his son Nathan. The kingship of Jesus does not come through Joseph's line. This is because God pronounced a curse on Jehoiachin, a descendent of Solomon and one of the last kings of Judah. Jehoiachin did evil and wicked things, so it was declared, "Write this man down as childless, a man who shall not succeed in his days, for none of his offspring shall succeed in sitting on the throne of David and ruling again in Judah" (Jeremiah 22:30). This declaration did not remove the promise God had given David. The promise remained, which is why we see that the kingship of Jesus came not through Joseph's line, but through his mother, Mary—still through the tribe of Judah and through David, but by way of Nathan instead of Solomon.

Jesus' kingship was established all the way back in David's time. The prophets spoke boldly about the fact that the Messiah would be a king. When the wise men were seeking to visit Jesus after He had been born, they said, "Where is he who has been born King of the Jews? For we saw his star when it rose and have come to worship him" (Matthew 2:2).

When Jesus was on trial before Pilate, Pilate asked Him if He was the King of the Jews. Jesus answered: "My kingdom is not of this world. If my kingdom were of this world, my servants would have been fighting, that I might not be delivered over to the Jews. But my kingdom is not from the world" (John 18:36). And when Jesus was crucified, a sign was hung over His head that said, "This is Jesus, the King of the Jews" (Matthew 27:37).

The label of kingship was attached to Jesus in the Old Testament by the prophets, before He was born; in His early years of life by the wise men; and in His adult life and His death by the Jewish religious leaders and the Romans. With the latter, some of it was intended as mockery, but ultimately, it was reality. Jesus' kingship was announced and lived out. He was the King.

Jesus' Kingship Brings Peace

Jesus' triumphal entry into Jerusalem laid out some details about what His kingship was going to bring. The people living in Jesus' time needed to know these details before they could decide how to respond to Him. Knowing these facts will also help us decide how to respond to His kingship.

We're going to focus on two of the most important details. The first is revealed in Matthew 21:1–5:

> *Now when they drew near to Jerusalem and came to Bethphage, to the Mount of Olives, then Jesus sent two disciples, saying to them, "Go into the village in front of you, and immediately you will find a donkey tied, and a colt with her. Untie them and bring them to me. If anyone says anything to you, you shall say, 'The Lord needs them,' and he will send them at once." This took place to fulfill what was spoken by the prophet, saying, "Say to the daughter of Zion, 'Behold, your king is coming to you, humble, and mounted on a donkey, on a colt, the foal of a beast of burden.'"*

Let's process this for a moment. On the way to Jerusalem, Jesus had told His twelve disciples that when they reached the city, He would be arrested, beaten, and put to death by crucifixion and would then rise again (Matthew 20:17–19). This was not the first time He had told them this, but they still had trouble understanding.

Before they entered Jerusalem, Jesus asked two of His disciples to bring Him a donkey to ride on. Then, the scene of the triumphal entry began to unfold. But all of this was spoken centuries before by the prophets. Zechariah, who was one of the twelve minor prophets, proclaimed two especially important things in his short book: he proclaimed that a king was coming, and he proclaimed how the king was going to come.

Zechariah 9:9 begins, "Rejoice greatly, O daughter of Zion! Shout aloud, O daughter of Jerusalem! Behold, your king is coming to you." The people listening to Zechariah would have been stuck in their own times, in their present moment. Zechariah prophesied to Jewish exiles who had returned from Babylon to rebuild Jerusalem and the temple, so they would have been imagining a king who would come and re-establish Israel not only as a nation but as a dominant nation—a nation that sought vengeance against the Assyrians and the Babylonians for taking them captive.

Zechariah continued in the second half of verse 9: "Righteous and having salvation is he, humble and mounted on a donkey, on a colt, the foal of a donkey." The people would've been hoping for a king mounted on a warhorse, which would have indicated that he was a powerful conqueror.

But there's more to the word God gave Zechariah about this coming king. Verse 10 continues: "I will cut off the chariot from Ephraim and the war horse from Jerusalem; and the battle bow shall be cut off, and he shall speak peace to the nations; his rule shall be from sea to sea, and from the River to the ends of the earth." When the king comes, he is going to speak peace. Zechariah's audience would have been more interested in vengeance than peace.

Interestingly, Isaiah, who lived seven hundred years before Jesus was born, prophesied that Jesus would be called the Prince of Peace (Isaiah 9:6). Peace was also a major theme in Jesus' life. In John 14:1, He said, "Let not your hearts be troubled. Believe in God; believe also in me." Even though He came to bring peace, He understood that there is a heart issue—and that there has been a heart issue ever since Adam and Eve. Also, His peace is not just being friendly and kind to one another. The peace He brings is an internal peace, a peace that will heal our hearts, which are darkened and in turmoil because of sin.

Jesus said in John 14:27, "Peace I leave with you; my peace I give to you. Not as the world gives do I give to you." We must ask *why* here. "Peace I leave with you; my peace I give to you." But *why?* Why is Jesus giving us peace? It's because of what the remainder of this verse says: "Let not your hearts be troubled, neither let them be afraid." He is giving us peace because our hearts have been the issue since the garden of Eden.

And so, when Jesus entered Jerusalem as prophesied by Zechariah, He was announcing He was a King who was going to bring peace. But even though Jesus is our King who brings us peace, we often persist in putting ourselves in toxic environments where there is no peace. If you're wondering why you don't have the peace Jesus offers, it's because you are not living under His authority as King and you're not putting yourself in a place where His kingship can offer you peace.

The story of Jesus' triumphal entry into Jerusalem continues in Matthew 21:6–11:

> *The disciples went and did as Jesus had directed them. They brought the donkey and the colt and put on them their cloaks, and he sat on them. Most of the crowd spread their cloaks on the road, and others cut branches from the trees and spread them on the road. And the crowds that went before him and that followed him were shouting, "Hosanna to the Son of David! Blessed is he who comes in the name of the Lord! Hosanna in the highest!" And when he entered Jerusalem, the whole city was stirred up, saying, "Who is this?" And the crowds said, "This is the prophet Jesus, from Nazareth of Galilee."*

The crowd was understandably excited. The prophecy of Zechariah was unfolding right in front of them. The people were cutting down tree branches to spread on the road and even spreading their own cloaks on the road, all the while shouting, "Hosanna!" which means, "Save us!"[22] They were living under the rule of the Romans, so they were looking for a vengeful king who would overthrow the Romans and re-establish Israel as a nation. But Jesus had already been proclaimed by the prophets to be a King who would bring peace.

Jesus' Kingship Brings Healing

In the midst of the crowds and the chaos, Jesus made His way through the city until He got to the temple. He then did the unthinkable: "And Jesus entered the temple and drove out all who sold and bought in the temple, and he overturned the tables of the money-changers and the seats of those who sold pigeons" (Matthew 21:12).

In those days, it was common practice for animals to be sold at the temple so people could purchase them and sacrifice them to atone for their sins.[23] Jesus walked into the temple and saw this, and He started flipping over tables: "He said to them, 'It is written, "My house shall be called a house of prayer," but you make it a den of robbers'" (Matthew 21:13). Here, Jesus was fulfilling another prophecy and revealing a second important detail about His kingship. Read Isaiah 56:6–8:

> *"And the foreigners who join themselves to the LORD, to minister to him, to love the name of the LORD, and to be his servants, everyone who keeps the Sabbath and does not profane it, and holds fast my covenant—these I will bring to my holy mountain, and make them joyful in my house of prayer; their burnt offerings and their sacrifices will be accepted on my altar; for my house shall be called a house of prayer for all peoples." The Lord GOD, who gathers the outcasts of Israel, declares, "I will gather yet others to him besides those already gathered."*

God created all people equal. I know that's an idea we've struggled with for a long time. We seem to have created a system in our minds and in our world in which there is a lack of equality among us as God's people. But God created us equal, and He created us for a purpose. This passage in Isaiah makes it clear, Jesus' kingship isn't just for the Jews. It's for all people—for anyone who will come to Him. It doesn't matter what your race or ethnicity is, or what your past or present is. His kingship is available to everyone, and His house will be called a house of prayer for all peoples.

Let's return to Matthew 21. Jesus was about to speak a detail that changed the entire environment He was in. Here's verse 14: "And the blind and the lame came to him in the temple, and he healed them." In the culture of that time, because of the Law and because of the way they had set up their religious rules and regulations, the blind, the lame, and the outcasts were not allowed to go into the temple because they were unclean.[24]

But when Jesus entered the temple and flipped over the tables, proclaiming that His house would be called a house of prayer, those people—the unclean—immediately knew their King had arrived. Not only was He going to speak peace, but He was also going to bring healing. Those who needed healing rushed to Him inside the temple even though they were not allowed to be there because they wanted to be in His presence.

Isaiah 35:4–6 is one of several prophecies about how the King will bring healing:

> *Say to those who have an anxious heart, "Be strong; fear not! Behold, your God will come with vengeance, with the recompense of God. He will come and save you." Then the eyes of the blind shall be opened, and the ears of the deaf*

> *unstopped; then shall the lame man leap like a deer, and the tongue of the mute sing for joy. For waters break forth in the wilderness, and streams in the desert.*

Those who were unclean heard the shouts of "Hosanna!" and saw Jesus entering the city on a donkey's colt. They saw Him enter the temple and start flipping over the tables of the money-changers, and they heard Him proclaim, "My house shall be called a house of prayer." They recognized the signs, and there was nothing that would stop them from coming into the presence of their King to receive healing and peace.

Have You Submitted to Jesus' Kingship?

And so, we have this beautiful moment in Scripture where Jesus' kingship was being announced in such a pure and simple way, declaring that He was bringing peace and healing. But many of us do not live in peace on a daily basis, and many of us are desperate for healing. Not only was Jesus' kingship announced here, but so was our path to submitting to His kingship. Yes, Jesus brings peace and healing, but how do we submit to His kingship so we can access those things?

The answer is in Matthew 21:13, when Jesus said, "My house shall be called a house of prayer." When He said this in the temple, everyone began to respond. This is what caused them to recognize their King, and it should cause us to recognize our King as well. Peace and healing come through prayer. Jesus' kingship comes when we bow our heads and pray, submitting to His kingship.

There is something so powerfully wrong with what's happening in many believers' lives today. It's because we claim Jesus is our Lord and our King, but we refuse to submit to His authority. And that is because we are not people who seek peace and healing through prayer. We're looking for immediate solutions and instant gratification, for something else that can give us peace, for a way to heal ourselves. But Jesus tells us we can only receive peace and healing through prayer. Why? Because when we pray, we are acknowledging He is our King and He is the only One who can give these things to us.

May we not just claim Jesus as our King. May we also place our lives under His kingship, where we can be reconciled back to God.

WORKBOOK

Chapter Eight Questions

Question: How is Jesus different from the rulers, kings, and leaders of the world? Is there evidence of His kingship in your life and your heart? What areas of your life still need Jesus' peace and healing?

____

____

____

____

____

____

____

____

____

____

____

Action: Have you submitted your life to Jesus' authority? Is He king in your life? Does His peace reign in you? If not, make a list of things to which you give authority in your life. Which of those areas could you begin to de-throne?

____

____

____

____

____

____

____

____

____

____

____

____

Chapter Eight Notes

CHAPTER NINE

The Church

The eighth marker that will help us to navigate through Scripture is the church. As a pastor, I have discovered that many people in the church think the church exists to serve their needs. That is not a biblical understanding of the church. The Bible teaches that the call of the church is to take the gospel to the ends of the earth, and how we accomplish this is by living out the expression of Christ's love.

I went to Dallas Baptist University for my degree. While there, I played for their soccer team, was married, and working several jobs. One of the jobs I had was serving as a youth pastor. One day I was particularly distracted by the many things happening—a test, preparing a message for youth group, and the mundane daily tasks that piled up. I had been preparing a message about Jesus washing the feet of His disciples.

I was walking across campus with my mind jumping between the test, my message for youth group, and what I was going to eat for lunch. As I rushed across campus, I walked past a statue I had seen hundreds of times, but this time it stopped me in my tracks. The statue was of Jesus washing the feet of a disciple. I froze and just looked at it.

It clicked inside my heart that I was looking at the purpose of the church. The church is the expression of Christ's love in action. As we dig into Scripture, this visual must stay prevalent. The visual of this statue does not take away our call to reach the nations, but simply gives us the blueprint for executing it.

Let's take a look at the passage in which the church was founded, Matthew 16:13–17:

> *Now when Jesus came into the district of Caesarea Philippi, he asked his disciples, "Who do people say that the Son of Man is?" And they said, "Some say John the Baptist, others say Elijah, and others Jeremiah or one of the prophets." He said to them, "But who do you say that I am?" Simon Peter replied, "You are the Christ, the Son of the living God." And Jesus answered him, "Blessed are you, Simon Bar-Jonah! For flesh and blood has not revealed this to you, but my father who is in heaven."*

You may be wondering why Jesus referred to Simon Peter as "Simon Bar-Jonah." "Bar" means "son of", and the name Jonah can be translated as John. Jesus is therefore referring to him as "Simon, son of John."[25] Jesus was emphasizing that His identity as Messiah was not revealed to Peter by Peter's earthly father. It was revealed to him by God, who is Jesus' heavenly father. Jesus was putting a divide between heaven and earth by declaring that there are things heaven will expose that the earth cannot. Simon Peter's earthly father could not have explained these things to him. Only the Father who is in heaven could do that, and Simon Peter was blessed to have encountered Him in that way.

Jesus continued speaking to Simon Peter in Matthew 16:18: "And I tell you, you are Peter, and on this rock I will build my church, and the gates of hell shall not prevail against it." It needs to be clarified here that Jesus was not saying Peter himself was the rock on which the church would be built. Rather, the rock in question was Peter's confession that Jesus is the Messiah. Jesus was and is the cornerstone on which the church is built (Ephesians 2:19–21).

Evidence that the church is not built on Peter can be seen a few verses later, in Matthew 16:21–23:

> *From that time Jesus began to show his disciples that he must go to Jerusalem and suffer many things from the elders and chief priests and scribes, and be killed, and on the third day be raised. And Peter took him aside and began to rebuke him, saying, "Far be it from you, Lord! This shall never happen to you." But he turned and said to Peter, "Get behind me, Satan! You are a hindrance to me. For you are not setting your mind on the things of God, but on the things of man."*

Jesus was telling Peter he was getting in the way of God's plan. He then told Peter to get behind Him. A little bit later in Matthew 26, Jesus forewarned that all His disciples would fall away from Him. Then Jesus and Peter had this exchange in verses 33–34:

> *Peter answered him, "Though they all fall away because of you, I will never fall away." Jesus said to him, "Truly, I tell you, this very night, before the rooster crows, you will deny me three times."*

We see Jesus' words play out in Matthew 26:69–75. Yet we also saw, in Matthew 16:18, Jesus saying to Peter, "On this rock I will build my church." The church belongs to Jesus, and He established it on Peter's confession of Jesus' name.

The Church Is to Follow Jesus' Example

While Jesus lived on the earth, He determined how the church was going to function and guided His disciples to live according to His example. First and foremost, He called them to be a people of prayer. Not only did He flip over the tables of the money-changers in the temple and proclaim, "My house shall be called a house of prayer," (Matthew 21:13), but He also prayed with His disciples and prayed for them. He even prayed for us as future believers. Jesus made it clear, if the church is going to be the hope of the world, the power source that comes from a holy and righteous God, then we will need to seek God's power. We will need to seek Him to move by requesting it through prayer.

Jesus modeled prayer for the church, and He also demonstrated that the church would be known for its love. You may have been wronged or hurt by people in a church, and that may have led you to believe the church is unloving. Jesus, however, illustrated love by loving the unlovable. There was no sinner, no outcast, whom Jesus would not pursue and love.

When Jesus was asked about the greatest commandment, He gave this response: "You shall love the Lord your God with all your heart and with all your soul and with all your mind. This is the great and first commandment. And a second is like it: You shall love your neighbor as yourself" (Matthew 22:37–39). We live in a day where people hate more than they love. The church should emulate Jesus and love recklessly.

Next, Jesus modeled for the church the necessity of baptism. He received baptism, even though He never sinned (Matthew 3:13–17). Why? Because He wanted the church to understand it was important and to imitate Him. He instituted the Lord's Supper and showed the church what it should look like (Luke 22:19–20). Paul made sure the early church followed the model that Jesus established for the Lord's Supper and cleared up any questions they had about it in his first letter to the Corinthians (1 Corinthians 11:17–34).

Jesus also equipped and sent out His disciples. In Matthew 28:19–20, He said to them, "Go therefore and make disciples of all nations, baptizing them in the name of the Father and of the Son and of the Holy Spirit, teaching them to observe all that I have commanded you. And behold, I am with you always, to the end of the age." This is not a command that Jesus gave specifically to missionaries. This is a command to the church. Missionary work and church work are not two separate things. We're all here to reach people for Christ and to equip believers to be more like Him. We've set up a divide here, but Jesus makes it clear that there is no divide. We are all called to be the hands and feet of a holy and righteous God.

We are ambassadors of Christ, and the gospel is our heartbeat. The Good News of the salvation that Christ brought to this world should roll off the lips of every believer. Equipping the saints to propel the gospel to the ends of the world is not part of some divine wish-list; it is a command from Jesus. This command requires us to live on mission, and that mission is not accomplished without our hearts, our minds, and our resources.

Jesus repeatedly addressed giving throughout the Gospels. We need to support the church financially in its mission because there is so much work to be done in this world, and without resources, that work doesn't happen.

Community Is Essential to the Church

After Jesus finished equipping the church, He sent them to live out the church in community. The church was founded on a confession; Jesus' example guided and taught them; and then, Jesus sent them out into the community. Why is community so important?

Acts 2:42 tells us of the early church, "And they devoted themselves to the apostles' teaching and the fellowship, to the breaking of bread and the prayers." Jesus had already illustrated these four things to His disciples. The church had been established, and now it was functioning—and it still is!

Let's focus for a moment on the apostles' teachings. The apostles taught publicly so that the doctrine would be guarded. If doctrine is not guarded, and people only learn about Scripture on their own instead of in a community like the church, false doctrine will emerge.

The church today is struggling because the doctrine has not been guarded. As a result, pastors all over the world give you their thoughts and opinions—how you can be wealthy, how you can be happy—instead of God's truth. People listen and agree with them and think they're hearing good, biblically solid teaching. But the doctrine of the Bible was not being preached, nor was it being protected. And that is because the church doesn't know the doctrine to protect.

We teach publicly in order to guard the doctrine. As a pastor, I sometimes make mistakes in my preaching and teaching. People always reach out to correct me, and I welcome that correction because I want Scripture to be guarded. Protecting the doctrine of Scripture is much more important to me than protecting my pride and my ego. And that's our responsibility as a church.

The early church also devoted themselves to fellowship. In this day and age, we tend to think of fellowship as fun activities that church members can do together to get better acquainted and enjoy each other's company. We go bowling together, or we throw a Super Bowl party. But there's more to fellowship. Fellowship refers to a connection so deep, it's like your souls are connected. You care about each other so that when one person cries, everyone cries with them. When one person has a need, everyone works to fill it. There was an intentional connection among the members of the early church.

This type of connection is missing from the church today. You may feel like you don't need more friends, but you do need people who will challenge you and biblically discipline you when you're out of step, and who will speak into you so you can do what God has put you on this earth to do. That's what fellowship should be. It's about caring for each other's needs, spiritual and physical.

Fellowship in the church is broken today because of our own selfishness. We know people in our church have needs, but we just don't want to take care of those needs. We ignore other people's needs because we want to indulge ourselves. This violates the very spirit of Acts 2:42.

When my wife and I first got married, she bought me an expensive watch as a gift. It cost two thousand dollars. I was a youth pastor at the time, and the youth group and I were helping out a single mother with two kids by putting shingles on her house. It was raining that day, so we covered the house with tarps to protect it until we could work on it. The mother asked me if we could keep part of the house covered with tarps for a while so that instead of spending all her money buying the shingles, she could use some of it to buy groceries. She didn't have any money to buy food for her kids for the week.

I gathered everyone together so that we could pray for her need. As we were praying, I looked down and realized that my expensive watch was on the same hand that was holding the hand of this single mother who couldn't even feed her kids. I was so guilt-stricken and convicted that when I got home, I took the watch off and stuck it in a drawer. I never wore it again.

Do you know what this selfish idiot never even considered? Selling it and giving her the money. That's why Jesus said, "For where your treasure is, there your heart will be also" (Matthew 6:21). I didn't have fellowship with this woman. My spirit wasn't connected with hers. I wanted to pray over her need, but I didn't want to meet her need. I did nothing for her; I only took off my watch and never wore it again so that I would feel less guilty.

That's human nature, though. God convicts us about something, and we feel a little guilty, so we step back a bit. We take measures to keep ourselves from feeling guilty, but we don't really engage with what God has convicted us about. And when we do that, we break the spirit of biblical fellowship. So, to keep the spirit of fellowship, I'm not suggesting that we can't have nice things, but I am contending that we can't ignore the nudges God gives us. When He says to take care of our brother or sister, we do so, to keep the spirit of true biblical fellowship.

The early church also devoted themselves to the breaking of bread. Some scholars think this means they took communion every time they gathered together, while some scholars think it means they ate a meal when they gathered together because they were a family and families eat together. Others claim that the reason the early church broke bread every time they met together was because there were people who belonged to the church who didn't have any food, and the church wanted to make sure everyone was taken care of.[26] [27] Because that's what the church does.

If the modern church had been doing its part to take care of people, I wonder if we would have as many government programs providing for the poor, the sick, and the elderly. We are told in James 1:27, "Religion that is pure and undefiled before God the Father is this: to visit orphans and widows in their affliction, and to keep oneself unstained from the world." If the church were doing its job, maybe the government wouldn't have to pick up the slack.

Lastly, the early church devoted themselves to prayer. We see the result of this devotion to prayer in the next verse, Acts 2:43: "And awe came upon every soul, and many wonders and signs were being done through the apostles." Why was there a powerful movement happening? Because of prayer. When there is no prayer, there are no miracles. There is no power. We are God's people, and we should be seeking His hand to move in all circumstances. That's what the early church did.

Acts 2:44–45 continues, "And all who believed were together and had all things in common. And they were selling their possessions and belongings and distributing the proceeds to all, as any had need." The early church didn't hide their possessions in drawers and feel guilty about them. They sold them and gave that money to all who had need. The early churched functioned in community, meeting the needs of the people around them. They overcame the selfishness that pushes us to meet our own needs and fill our own pockets, our own closets, and our own garages, asking themselves instead what they could do for other people.

In the church today, it's so easy for us to gather every Sunday and pretend people around us don't have needs. If we were truly people who believe we need to give to the work of God and take care of each other, we would never have a need go unfilled, and we would be able to reach more people for Christ.

Are You a Guest or a Host?

The church was established on a confession, and Jesus set the example of what the church should be. He then sent the church out to live in community, to care for each other and walk in fellowship with each other, so that everyone's physical and spiritual needs would be met. That is what Jesus wants from the church. Today, however, the church has become something else.

Here's our reality: when it comes to the church, you're either a host or a guest. A guest is someone who can arrive late and leave early. A guest is someone who sees a piece of trash on the floor and doesn't pick it up because it's not their responsibility. They open their bulletin and see the request for volunteers to help with various ministries, and they ignore it because, after all, they're just a guest. They aren't invested in what's happening at that church.

A host, on the other hand, arrives early to confirm that everything is ready and to serve others. They leave late because they're making sure everyone and everything are taken care of. A host picks up the stray piece of trash they see on the floor and volunteers to fill needed roles in the church. They're eager to do whatever they can because they want to be part of that church. A host confesses Jesus as their Lord and Savior, follows His example, and chooses to live out their part in their church community. They give to their church, they serve their church, and they invest in their church.

Don't be a guest. Be a host. The church is your home. Be there to welcome others and to meet their needs, as Christ would have us do.

WORKBOOK

Chapter Nine Questions

Question: What is the church? What was the purpose of establishing the church on the earth? As part of the church, are you emulating the example Christ set for His church (praying, loving recklessly, being baptized, participating in the Lord's Supper, living on mission, giving generously)? Which area from this list do you most need to grow in?

____

____

____

____

____

____

____

____

____

Action: Are you a part of a church community that cares for each other and walks in fellowship with each other so everyone's physical and spiritual needs can be met? As part of the church, you are the expression of Christ to the world. Whose needs can you meet this month, this week, and this day? To whom do you need to reach out with a phone call or a visit? Write down the name of a specific person and intentional ways to serve that person.

Chapter Nine Notes

CHAPTER TEN

The Promise of Jesus' Return

The ninth and final marker that will help us to navigate through Scripture is the promise of Jesus' return.

I was twenty-one years old, standing on the porch of a resort in Ocho Rios, Jamaica, waiting for my soon-to-be bride to come through the doors. I fell in love with Kristina when I was sixteen. For five years, I had chased her, loved her, and honored her. This was the day of my dreams, and at that point in my life, the most exciting day.

I stood there waiting and waiting and waiting, and the wait seemed unbearable. Bear in mind that I was outside in a tropical environment wearing a tuxedo. Between the excitement, the humidity, and the tuxedo, I was sweating bullets and becoming impatient. I sent someone to find out what was taking so long, only to find out my precious bride was waiting for a specific song to walk out to.

After what seemed like forever, the door finally opened, and I saw my beautiful bride standing there in all her glory. I can tell you right now, I have no idea what song was playing. Everything I had been waiting for was right in front of my eyes, and that's all that mattered.

The church is waiting for Christ to return, and one day we will see Him in all of His glory right before our eyes. When Jesus established the church, He gave her the promise that He will come back for her. This is one of the things that separates Christianity from all other religions. Other religions are about man trying to reach God, but Christianity is about God coming to us.

We see God's presence throughout the Old Testament described as a cloud. We see it hovering over Mount Sinai when Moses received the Ten Commandments (Exodus 19:9). God's presence led the Israelites through the wilderness in the form of a pillar of cloud by day and a pillar of fire by night (Exodus 13:21–22). Once the tabernacle—the tent of meeting where the Israelites would worship God—was established in the wilderness, the cloud of God's presence filled the tent (Exodus 40:34–38). And when the construction of the temple was completed, the glory of God's presence filled the temple (1 Kings 8:10–11). God's presence came down to be with His people.

In the New Testament, this continued with the birth of Jesus Christ, the Son of God, in Bethlehem (Luke 1:30–33). God's presence was with His people on earth through Jesus, who lived a sinless life and died a sacrificial death on Calvary's cross to take the punishment for our sins and restore our relationship with God. Then He was taken down from the cross and placed in a borrowed, empty tomb, which was sealed. His disciples were in despair, believing that all hope had been lost. But on the third day, Jesus rose from the dead. He spent another forty days on earth, and at the end of those forty days, He ascended to heaven in view of His disciples. And once again, we see the cloud of God's presence.

Acts 1:6 says of Jesus' disciples, "So when they had come together, they asked him, 'Lord, will you at this time restore the kingdom to Israel?'" Jesus had just died on the cross for their sins and risen from the dead, and now He was about to ascend to the Father. And His disciples were asking Him if He was going to be king now and overthrow the Romans. Even after all this, they were still desiring an earthly king.

Jesus responded to them in Acts 1:7–8, "It is not for you to know times or seasons that the Father has fixed by his own authority. But you will receive power when the Holy Spirit has come upon you, and you will be my witnesses in Jerusalem and in all Judea and Samaria, and to the end of the earth." Jesus was explaining to His disciples that this was not about a kingship on earth. It was about a bigger kingdom. He also told them that even though He was leaving them, God would send them the Holy Spirit.

The Holy Spirit dwells inside God's people, and He leads us, guides us, and corrects us. He gives us strength on a daily basis, and He separates us from the rest of the world and sets us apart for Himself.

Acts 1:9–11 continues:

> *And when he had said these things, as they were looking on, he was lifted up, and a cloud took him out of their sight. And while they were gazing into heaven as he went, behold, two men stood by them in white robes, and said, "Men of Galilee, why do you stand looking into heaven? This Jesus, who was taken up from you into heaven, will come in the same way as you saw him go into heaven."*

This was a great moment in Scripture because the disciples were standing there in awe. Two angels were trying to get their attention to redirect them toward the commission Jesus had just given them, to be His witnesses throughout the world. It was time for them to start being the church.

The disciples, however, were focused on Jesus' return. He had promised that He would come back, and that could happen at any moment. How long would it be? What if they missed it? But Jesus made it clear: they weren't supposed to just stand around waiting for Him. They needed to be doing God's work, and sharing God's love and Jesus' story, with other people.

Jesus' Return Will Be Impossible to Miss

But how can we be confident that we haven't missed Jesus' return? It's because John, one of Jesus' twelve close disciples, who is also known as John the Revelationist, wrote the book of Revelation. According to Tertullian, an early church leader, John was persecuted for being a follower of Jesus. As a result, he was banished to the island of Patmos. While he was on Patmos, he had a vision of God speaking to him. John recorded this vision in the book of Revelation.[28]

In the book of Revelation, God made it clear we have not missed His return and the whole world will know about it when He comes back. Revelation 19:11–16 tells us this about Jesus' return to earth:

> *Then I saw heaven opened, and behold, a white horse! The one sitting on it is called Faithful and True, and in righteousness he judges and makes war. His eyes are like a flame of fire, and on his head are many diadems, and he has a name written that no one knows but himself. He is clothed in a robe dipped in blood, and the name by which he is called is The Word of God. And the armies of heaven, arrayed in fine linen, white and pure, were following him on white horses. From his mouth comes a sharp sword with which to strike down the nations, and he will rule them with a rod of iron. He will tread the winepress of the fury of the wrath of God the Almighty. On his robe and on his thigh he has a name written, King of kings and Lord of lords.*

This is the picture John was given regarding Jesus' return. Through the book of Revelation, God reassures the church that there is no way we will miss it when Jesus comes back. We should therefore not be deceived by false reports that Jesus has already returned. Jesus said in Matthew 24:36 that only God knows the day and the hour of Jesus' return. Even Jesus Himself doesn't know. As such, the church doesn't need to be focused on figuring out the date and time. We should be focused on doing God's work.

Jesus is returning as a warrior dressed for battle, accompanied by the armies of heaven. The only ones who are protected from His wrath are those who have submitted to His kingship by accepting Him as their Lord and Savior, and who therefore have been redeemed by the blood He shed on the cross for their sins. Those who have rejected the cross, who have rejected Scripture and the truth, will not be spared.

The only ones who are protected from God's wrath are those who are hidden in Christ. That's why Scripture tells us that there is no condemnation for those who are in Christ Jesus (Romans 8:1). His judgment will pass over us because we are His children. This was foreshadowed in the Old Testament (Exodus 12). It is yet to come, but we can be certain that it's on its way.

Jesus Will Come Back for His Bride

Jesus also promised He will return, in John 14. He began in verse 1: "Let not your hearts be troubled. Believe in God; believe also in me." Throughout this book, we have discussed how sin is a heart issue. The sin in the garden of Eden wasn't necessarily Adam and Eve's disobedience in eating the fruit; it was that they desired God's authority to determine right and wrong. There was a problem with their hearts.

The Law was established for their hearts. The judges entered the picture, but because the judges had dark, wicked hearts, so did the people. The kings came on the scene, but they divided and destroyed everything—again, because of this heart issue. The prophets then came and declared that Jesus was going to come and fix this heart issue. Therefore, when Jesus spoke the words, "Let not your hearts be troubled," He was saying, "I am here! Put your faith in Me and in what I am saying to you."

Jesus continued in John 14:2–3, "In my Father's house are many rooms. If it were not so, would I have told you that I go to prepare a place for you? And if I go and prepare a place for you, I will come again and will take you to myself, that where I am you may be also." In the Jewish culture of Jesus' day, this would have been the equivalent of getting down on one knee with a ring box in your hand. This was a marriage proposal.[29]

A massive feast would be held, and there would be four specially positioned cups of wine. The hopeful suitor would take one of the cups, bring it to the young lady in question, and speak to her these words: "In my father's house, there are many rooms. If it were not so, I would not have told you. I will go prepare a place for you, and when it is prepared, I will come back for you. Will you drink of this cup?" If she drank from the cup, she was accepting his proposal.[30]

The man would then immediately leave and start building an addition onto his father's house for his new bride. Once the addition was completed, he would return for his bride. They would move into their new home, and for a year, the new husband would be exempt from working and fighting in wars so the couple could simply focus on being married.[31]

Jesus was saying He is the groom, the church is His bride, and He will, without a doubt, be back for her. These are powerful statements.

The Timing of Jesus' Return

Much like the bride-to-be sitting anxiously at home and wondering when her husband would come for her, the church has been wondering when Jesus will come back for her since the moment He left. We continue to wait, with no idea when He will return. But that doesn't stop us from guessing. There are all sorts of books written about when Jesus will come back, and everyone has an opinion on the matter.

Part of the reason for this guessing is, Jesus has left us little pieces of information about His return in Scripture, and people have interpreted these in different ways. Take Matthew 24:33–34, for example, where Jesus said, "So also, when you see all these things, you know that he is near, at the very gates. Truly, I say to you, this generation will not pass away until all these things take place." "These things" refers to the signs of the end times.

What did Jesus mean when He said that "this generation will not pass away until all these things take place"? Skeptics would say that "this generation" has already passed away, but it's important to note that the Greek word translated as *generation* here is also the word for *race*.[32] When we think of a generation, we tend to think of layers of family—son, father, grandfather—but *generation* here means a whole "race," or people. Scripture describes all who have accepted Jesus as their Lord and Savior as "a chosen race, a royal priesthood, a holy nation, a people for his own possession, that you may proclaim the excellencies of him who called you out of darkness into his marvelous light" (1 Peter 2:9). All of God's people constitute one holy race, regardless of the color of their skin.

What Jesus was saying, therefore, is that this holy race—Christians—will not pass away before He returns. As the signs of the end times are taking place, there will still be Christians on this earth. That is what Matthew 24:33–34 is pointing to.

Look at Matthew 16:28, in which Jesus said, "Truly, I say to you, there are some standing here who will not taste death until they see the Son of Man coming in his kingdom." This is another verse skeptics and concerned Christians alike point to, asking if Jesus' return already happened because Jesus said some of the people standing there would not taste death until He came back.

The verse's context helps to explain its meaning. Right after Matthew 16:28, we read these words in Matthew 17:1–3:

> *And after six days Jesus took with him Peter and James, and John his brother, and led them up a high mountain by themselves. And he was transfigured before them, and his face shone like the sun, and his clothes became white as light. And behold, there appeared to them Moses and Elijah, talking with him.*

What Jesus was saying in Matthew 16:28 was, some of His disciples would see the power of His kingdom before they died. Six days later, that is exactly what happened for Peter, James, and John when they saw a bit of His glory unveiled and saw Him conversing with Moses and Elijah. They thought His kingdom had arrived, but Jesus was only giving them a glimpse of what is to come.

Jesus' Return Will Be Unexpected

Since John was the last person to receive a vision from God in Scripture, a lot of people look at Revelation 22 for indications of when Jesus will return. In Revelation 22:12,

Jesus proclaimed, "Behold, I am coming soon, bringing my recompense with me, to repay each one for what he has done." The word translated as "soon" is the Greek word *tachy*. It can mean "quickly," and it can also mean "suddenly."[33] Every time Jesus spoke of His return, He used that Greek word, and it seems He used it to mean "unexpectedly." Jesus told His disciples that His coming would be unexpected.

In Matthew 24:37–44, Jesus said to His disciples:

> *For as were the days of Noah, so will be the coming of the Son of Man. For as in those days before the flood they were eating and drinking, marrying and giving in marriage, until the day when Noah entered the ark, and they were unaware until the flood came and swept them all away, so will be the coming of the Son of Man. Then two men will be in the field; one will be taken and one left. Two women will be grinding at the mill; one will be taken and one left. Therefore, stay awake, for you do not know on what day your Lord is coming. But know this, that if the master of the house had known in what part of the night the thief was coming, he would have stayed awake and would not have let his house be broken into. Therefore you also must be ready, for the Son of Man is coming at an hour you do not expect.*

When we think of being ready for Jesus' return, we tend to think of whether we have accepted Jesus as Lord and Savior. Accepting Jesus is the best way to be ready. In this context, however, being ready means being aware that Jesus is going to return and that His return will happen unexpectedly. You'll be working with another person, and one of you will be taken and one of you will be left. And maybe the outcome for that person would've been different if you had taken the time to share with them about Jesus.

Here, being ready means actively telling other people about Jesus. And in order for us to tell other people about Jesus, we need to know Jesus, and we cannot know Jesus without reading and studying God's Word. It's one thing to say we believe in Jesus. It's another to actually follow Him. And we cannot be faithful followers of Jesus unless we are pursuing His Word.

Alpha and Omega (the Beginning and the End)

With any great story, the writer knows the ending before he starts. A great story tells the truth. God's story connected through nine defining markers leads us not to the end of a story, but to a new beginning. Jesus gave the church the promise of His return. The book of Revelation gives us the insight of the end becoming the beginning. The new earth described in Revelation 21, when Jesus returns, matches the picture we already read in Genesis, where there was a physical, perfect place with perfect communion between Him and His creation.

The new earth promised will also be a physical place where that perfection will exist again. It will be a spiritual, physical, and dimensional earth on which we will live for eternity in God's presence. There will be no death, no sickness, no sin, no tears, and no separation from God. Those who accept Christ in faith have the promise of an eternal home in the presence of God and will finally experience with joy the fullness of His glory. Amen, amen,

amen.

WORKBOOK

Chapter Ten Questions

Question: Are you ready for Jesus' return? What in your life is evidence that you are ready?

Action: Think of a person in your life you know you need to share Jesus with. Commit to telling them about Jesus as soon as possible. When the opportunity comes, be faithful to follow through.

Chapter Ten Notes

CONCLUSION

Let It Stick

My family went on a trip, our last family vacation before my wife and I became empty-nesters. We went to Glacier National Park in Montana and found a great hike. We were about thirty minutes into our hike when we ran into an incredible waterfall; it was truly breathtaking. At the bottom of the waterfall were massive rocks, which seemed to break up the stream that was flowing from the pool at the bottom of the waterfall.

The boulders looked like a massive natural dam. But the rushing water moved with ease around the boulders. The water, with force, moved its way down the mountain. We all stood in awe at the beauty and power of the flowing water. My wife broke the silence.

Standing on the cliff, looking down at the waterfall, she turned to our kids and said, "Just be water." She then explained, "The water always finds a way. That's my prayer for you two, that you always find a way."

For the next few days, we repeated the phrase, "Just be water," over and over. *"Just be water."* When we came home from our trip, the slogan continued for a few days, which turned into a few weeks.

Sometime after that, my son, who is a competitive golfer, was playing in a golf tournament. I was walking with another dad. Standing on the cart path and observing my son in a bit of a predicament, I said under my breath, but loud enough for him to hear, "Just be water." He gave a subtle smile, letting me know he understood what I had said. This simple phrase just stuck.

As I put together the content for the nine markers, this was the goal: that the nine markers will stick. The things that stick with us help us. The things that stick with us shape us. Now that you've read through this book, I hope these nine markers stick and create an understanding of the big picture of the Bible for you. I hope that the markers and themes in this book become placeholders helping you navigate through the Bible.

The nine markers we covered started in the beginning, when 1) God created. Then 2) sin happened, which 3) caused the Law to be established. Someone had to oversee the Law, so 4) judges were raised up by God. The people didn't want judges; they wanted kings, so 5) God gave them kings. Then the kings divided the nations, and the people strayed from God. So 6) God brought the prophets, who proclaimed the King of kings was coming; 7) Jesus did come. Then 8) the church was established, and Jesus promised to 9) return for His bride—the church.

If these nine markers stick with you, then no matter where you pick up in the Bible, you will have the foundation of structure and understanding to grasp the power of God's Word. You will know how He organized His story so you can step into it. May you fall in love with His story as you navigate it with the Nine!

REFERENCES

Notes

1. Bible Hub, "196. biblios." https://biblehub.com/greek/976.htm.

2. Edwards, Brian. *Nothing But the Truth.* Evangelical Press, 2006, p. 116–143.

3. McDowell, Josh. *Evidence That Demands a Verdict: Historical Evidences for the Christian Faith.* Volume 1. Thomas Nelson, 1979, p.65.

4. Miller, Stephen M. *How to Get into the Bible*. Thomas Nelson, 2012, p. 175.

5. Miller, *How to Get into the Bible,* p. 313.

6. Green, Jay P. *The Interlinear Bible Hebrew–Greek–English 4 Volume Edition with Strong's Concordance Numbers Above Each Word*. Hendrickson Publishers Marketing, 2005, p. 3.

7. Stone, Nathan. *Names of God*. Moody Publishers, 1987, p. 37.

8. Blue Letter Bible, "Strong's H3068 – *Yᵊhōvâ*." https://www.blue letterbible.org/lexicon/h3068/kjv/wlc/0-1/.

9. Blue Letter Bible, "Strong's H3068 – *Yəhōvâ*."

10. *The Interlinear Bible*. Vol. 4. Translated by Jay P. Green. Hendrickson, p. 290.

The Interlinear Bible. Vol. 3. Translated by Jay P. Green. Hendrickson, p. 1691.

11. *The Classic Midrash: Tannaitic Commentaries on the Bible*. Paulist Press, 1995.

12. *Holman Bible Dictionary: With Summary Definitions and Explanatory Articles on Every Bible Subject, Introductions and Teaching Outlines for Each Bible Book, In-depth Theological Articles, Plus Internal Maps, Charts, Illustrations, Scale Reconstruction Drawings, Archaeological Photos, and Atlas.* Holman Bible Publishers, 1991, p. 1357–1358.

Blue Letter Bible, "Strong's H8451 – *tôrâ*." https://www.blue letterbible.org/lexicon/h8451/kjv/wlc/0-1/.

13. American–Israeli Cooperative Enterprise. "Judaism: The 613 Mitzvot (Commandments)." Jewish Virtual Library. https://www.jewishvirtuallibrary.org/the-613-mitzvot-commandments.

14. Miller, *How to Get into the Bible,* p. 120.

15. Miller, *How to Get into the Bible,* p. 198.

16. *Holman Bible Dictionary,* p. 1172.

17. Walvoord, John F., and Roy B. Zuck. *The Bible Knowledge Commentary: Old Testament and New Testament.* David C. Cook, 2002, p. 510–512.

18. Miller, *How to Get into the Bible,* p. 198.

---

19. Based on a search of "know that I am the Lord" in the English Standard Version on Bible Gateway (https://www.biblegateway.com), excluding 16 results from books other than Ezekiel.

20. *Blue* Letter Bible, "Strong's H4186 – *môšāḇ*." https://www.blueletterbible.org/lexicon/h4186/kjv/wlc/0-1/.

21. Walvoord and Zuck, *The Bible Knowledge Commentary*, p. 1299.

22. Blue Letter Bible, "Strong's G5614 – *hōsanna*." https://www.blueletterbible.org/lexicon/g5614/kjv/tr/0-1/.

23. Arnold, Clinton E. *Zondervan Illustrated Bible Backgrounds Commentary: Matthew, Mark, Luke*. Zondervan, 2002, p.129.

24. Arnold, *Zondervan Illustrated Bible Backgrounds Commentary*, p. 130.

25. Blue Letter Bible, "Strong's G920 – *bariōna*." https://www.blueletterbible.org/lexicon/g920/kjv/tr/0-1/.

26. Keener, Craig S. *The IVP Bible Background Commentary: New Testament.* InterVarsity Press, 2014, p. 330.

27. Arnold, *Zondervan Illustrated Bible Backgrounds Commentary*, p. 237.

28. Tertullian. *The Prescription Against Heretics*. Blurb, 2020.

29. Vander Laan, Ray. "Marriage Cup Definition." https://www.thattheworldmayknow.com/define-marriage-cup.

30. Howard, Kevin, and Marvin Rosenthal. *The Feasts of the Lord.* Zion's Hope, 1996, p.16, 55.

31. Vander Laan, "Marriage Cup Definition."

32. Bible Hub, "1074. genea." https://biblehub.com/greek/1074.htm.

---

33. Blue Letter Bible, "Strong's G5035 – *tachy*." https://www.blueletterbible.org/lexicon/g5035/kjv/tr/0-1/.

About the Author

Believing the Bible reveals the nature and character of God, Donnie Smith has a passion to share that truth with people everywhere. Donnie is an expository Bible teacher using history, humor, and story to bring the Scriptures to life.

Donnie has served as a youth pastor, teaching pastor, and lead pastor over the past twenty-seven years. In 2009, he took the lead pastor role at The Fellowship in Round Rock, Texas. The Fellowship is a multi-site Bible teaching church. Donnie did both his undergraduate and graduate work at Dallas Baptist University.

Donnie is married to Kristina, and they have two children, Kylie and Clayton.

About Renown Publishing

Renown Publishing was founded with one mission in mind: to make your great idea famous.

At Renown Publishing, we don't just publish. We work hard to pair strategy with innovative marketing techniques so that your book launch is the start of something bigger.

Learn more at RenownPublishing.com.

Made in USA - Kendallville, IN